Chesthetica's Book of Chess Constructs

Original Computer-Generated Chess Problems for Solving and Analysis

Volume 4

by

Azlan Iqbal
College of Computing and Informatics
Universiti Tenaga Nasional
Malaysia

*For Amanda, Amber, Amy, Anna, Barbara, Britta, Cari, Caroline,
Chrissy, Cristina, Deanna, Elin, Elizabeth, Fareen, Gerri,
Jennifer, Jessica, Julia, Julia-Celine, Katryna, Katy, Laura, Leigh,
Lesley, Linda, Lori, Marguerite, Mia, Michelle, Molly, Natasha,
Rebecca, Sarah, Sasha, Thia, Wirda, Zely and Zoey.*

(MCMXCVII - MMIV)

ISBN 979-8651043583

Independently published.

2

Contents

INTRODUCTION

Thank you for reading this fourth volume of computer-generated chess problems by *Chesthetica*. This one features 80 original chess problems including mates in 3, mates in 4, mates in 5 and study-like constructs. Among the new elements you might have noticed is the size of the (printed) book, i.e. smaller so that it can be distributed more widely by the publisher; presumably you did not know size matters there. I actually tend to prefer the smaller size since it fits more snugly in the hand. One downside may be that the text, especially in some parts of the solutions chapter (due to editorial reasons), may require certain people to reach for a magnifying glass or the zoom feature of their smartphone camera.

Alternatively, at least with the e-book version, you may just click to see the online video solution where I simply explain it to you by moving the pieces on a board with some real time chess engine analysis to the side to prove it. Depending on how many years, decades, centuries or millennia after publication you are reading this, those videos may no longer be online or available, however; so forgive me in that regard. Each problem now also includes a brief description below the diagram about the material balance (or imbalance) and if a pawn promotion is close. This is to spare readers the trouble of calculating and noticing these aspects of the composition on their own. Whilst in most cases White may be ahead or even significantly ahead in material, it does not at all mean the problem is not challenging.

Even so, I do concede that a player having equal (or even better, less) material, yet winning, is often perceived as more aesthetically pleasing. Chess, even today, can be dynamic and paradoxical therefore it is difficult to put every position in a categorical box, especially when it comes to aesthetics. I am fairly confident most readers will find at least some of these problems as appealing as I did when I selected them. To be perfectly honest, my taste also changes (perhaps even 'improves') as the years go by so the types of compositions I select in the future may differ compared to say, the ones I selected for the first volume of this book series.

The solutions chapter is now more thorough or lengthy than before. Where there are multiple variations, I have included the full line with all the previous moves repeated. I believe this makes it easier to read and to identify alternative moves or variations in the solution. From a research perspective, there is still no 'solvability estimate' for studies that I could find or develop myself so you will notice that part missing in the studies, but noted for the forced mates like they were in the previous volume. There is a paper explaining how it works listed in the reference section at the end of this book, if you wish to learn more.

It is also perhaps worth noting that having received several requests from people to purchase *Chesthetica*, I am still not ready to commercialize it, if I ever will. I am not in any particular need for the (presumably meager) additional income. Besides, I believe it would take the resources of a much larger corporation to do a decent job of commercialization. Such an offer has yet materialized, if it ever will. If Chesthetica does get commercialized at some point, I cannot even imagine what wonders of chess composition some copies of it almost certainly will produce given the thousands or even millions running all over the world. For contrast, even all that has been produced thus far are from my copies alone running on just a few computers I can spare.

I was, however, contacted by someone (incidentally a doctorate, like myself) who was very interested in *Chesthetica's* compositions (*all of them*, in fact) and through a partnership they are now featured at his website. Some of them are also being used by a "chess for kids" online course to illustrate tactics and ideas in the game, for training purposes. I am glad therefore that *Chesthetica's* compositions have found some actual utility to potentially many thousands of people beyond being a source of pleasure or entertainment. Some people probably also use them to keep their brains active and healthier given that puzzle-solving is believed to help with this. With all that said, I hope you enjoy this volume as much or even more than the others.

Chapter 1

Selected Compositions Generated Between June and August 2016

In this first chapter you will find 13 computer-generated chess problems already covering the whole spectrum of compositions, i.e. forced mates (3, 4 and 5 moves) and a study-like construct. They also cover the whole spectrum of 'solvability', i.e. easy, moderate and difficult. Furthermore, there are positions where White has more, the same or less material than Black. None of this was planned in advance. It just so happened to be the case after the compositions were already selected for publication in the first chapter. So here alone you will already get a taste of what the whole book has to offer.

As I write this, I have already compiled *Chesthetica v11.71*. This version is notably different from earlier ones in that it incorporates 'quantum randomness', i.e. totally unpredictable numbers derived from the infinitesimal depths of the universe itself. By no means does *Chesthetica* place pieces on the board purely randomly. However, there are some aspects of randomness that were previously derived algorithmically, i.e. pseudorandom numbers. This made them theoretically predictable or subject to creating patterns over time. Though presently unproven, I and maybe a few others have perhaps already noticed some manifestations of this in the compositions generated thus far.

This is one of the main reasons I chose to test the idea of 'true' or quantum randomness since the technology was available and accessible. Incorporated and used in conjunction with the existing Digital Synaptic Neural Substrate (DSNS) computational creativity approach I developed, it might yield more interesting, challenging or aesthetically-pleasing compositions. I am in the midst of designing an experiment to test if the output of *Chesthetica* really is better using quantum randomness. If so, I will be sure to employ it from then onwards. It is generally important that the right balance of quality versus quantity is achieved. Not to mention optimal use of limited resources and time.

Computer-Generated Chess Problem 01071

White to Play and Mate in 3

Chesthetica v10.17 (Selangor, Malaysia)
Generated on 13 Jun 2016 at 7:29:56 PM
Solvability Estimate = Difficult

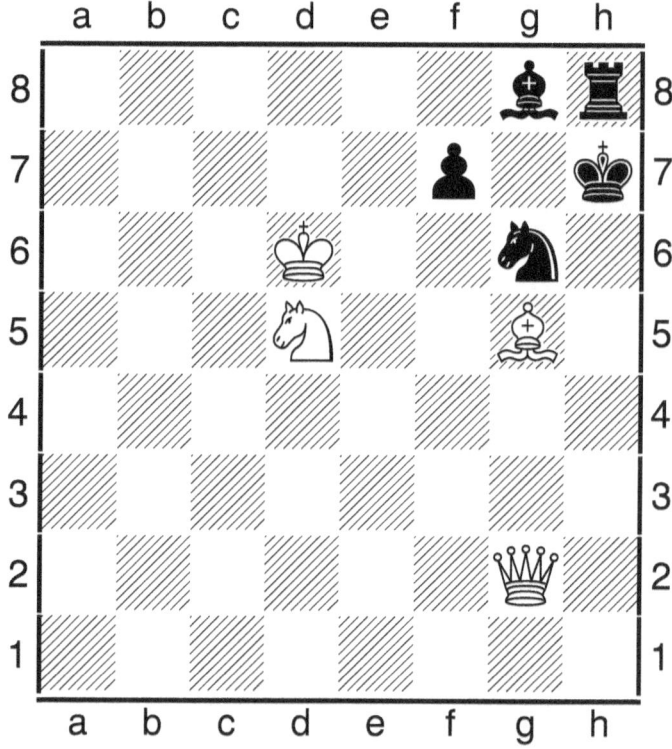

KQBN vs krbnp
White is ahead by three pawn units (one minor piece's worth) but
can you find the best way to proceed here?

Computer-Generated Chess Problem 01077

White to Play and Mate in 5
Chesthetica v10.17 (Selangor, Malaysia)
Generated on 16 Jun 2016 at 8:40:27 PM
Solvability Estimate = Easy

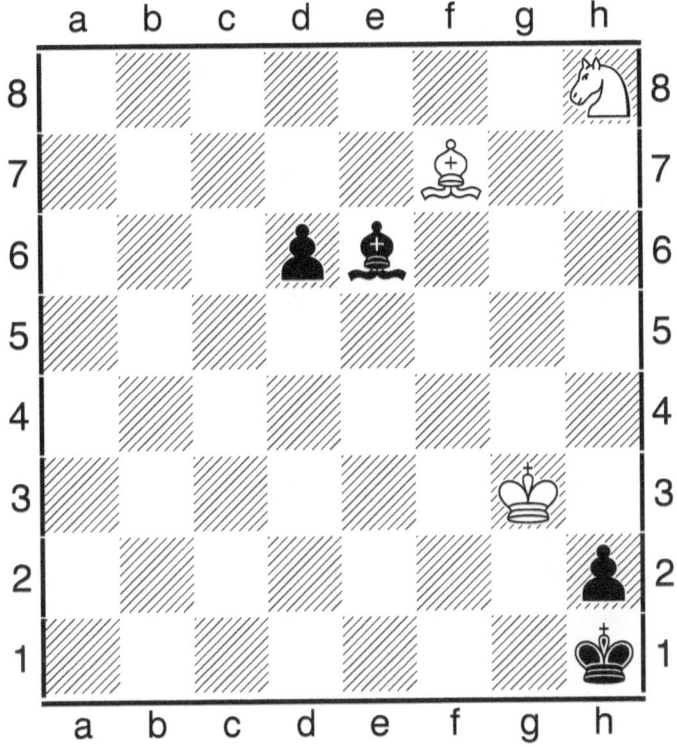

KBN vs kbpp
White is ahead by one pawn unit but can you find the best way to
proceed here? Black is also close to a pawn promotion.

Computer-Generated Chess Problem 01084

White to Play and Mate in 5
Chesthetica v10.17 (Selangor, Malaysia)
Generated on 23 Jun 2016 at 11:05:01 PM
Solvability Estimate = Difficult

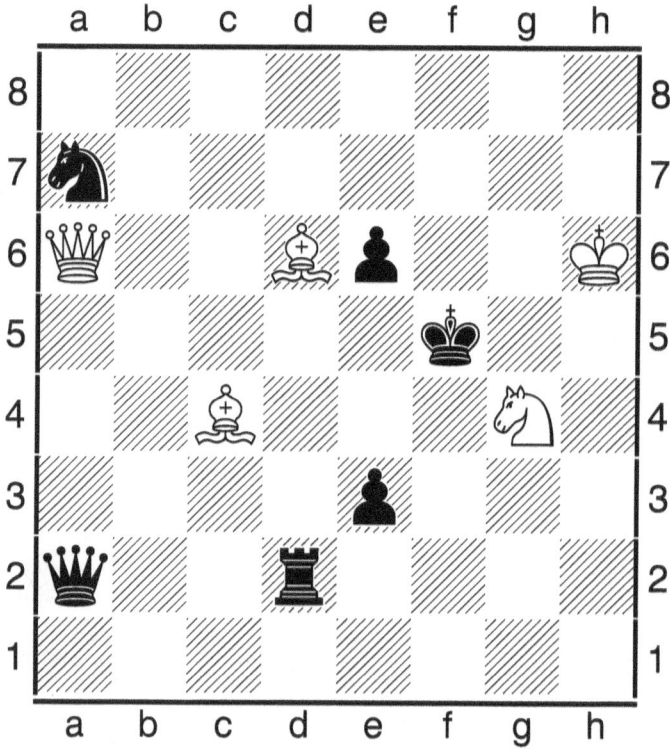

KQBBN vs kqrnpp
White is actually down by one pawn unit.

Computer-Generated Chess Problem 01091

White to Play and Mate in 5

Chesthetica v10.18 (Selangor, Malaysia)
Generated on 28 Jun 2016 at 1:56:56 AM
Solvability Estimate = Difficult

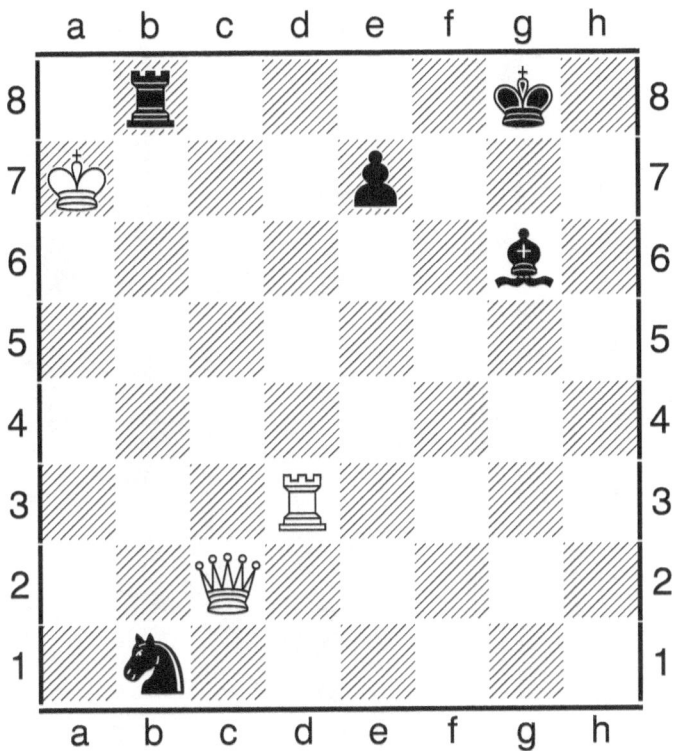

KQR vs krbnp
White is ahead by two pawn units but can you find the best way
to proceed here?

Computer-Generated Chess Problem 01104

White to Play and Win
Chesthetica v10.17 (Selangor, Malaysia)
Generated on 10 Jul 2016 at 6:53:21 PM

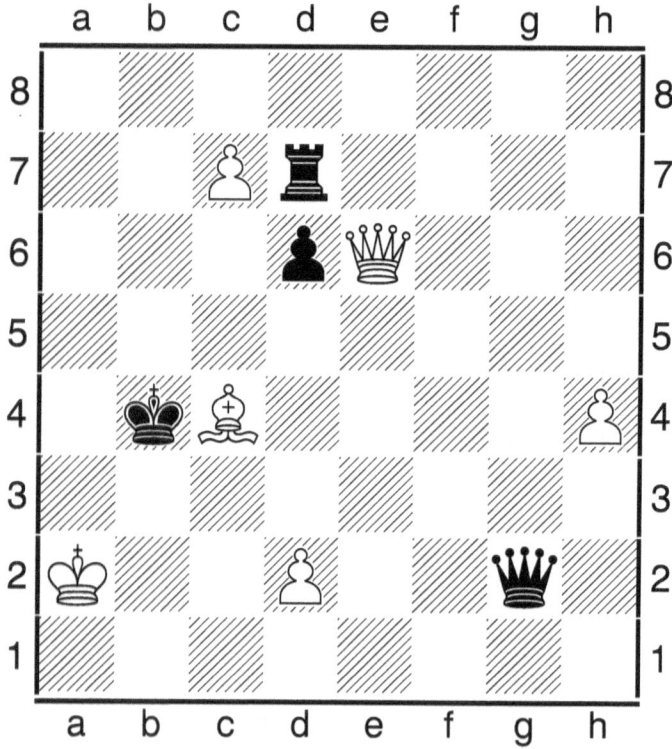

KQBPPP vs kqrp
White and Black have the same amount of material. White is also close to a pawn promotion.

Computer-Generated Chess Problem 01105

White to Play and Mate in 5
Chesthetica v10.17 (Selangor, Malaysia)
Generated on 10 Jul 2016 at 8:00:10 PM
Solvability Estimate = Moderate

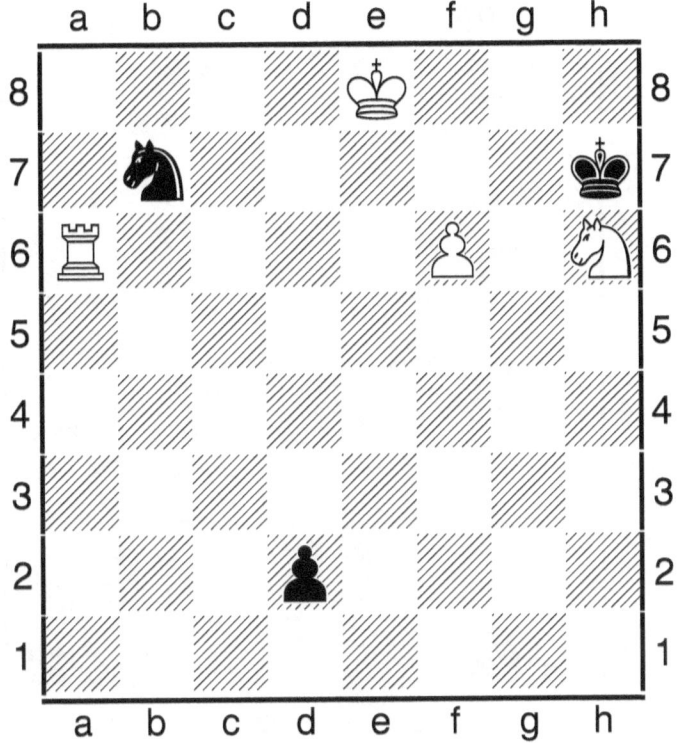

KRNP vs knp
White is ahead by five pawn units (a rook's worth) but can you find the best way to proceed here? Black is also close to a pawn promotion.

Computer-Generated Chess Problem 01107

White to Play and Mate in 4

Chesthetica v10.17 (Selangor, Malaysia)
Generated on 12 Jul 2016 at 1:36:55 AM
Solvability Estimate = Moderate

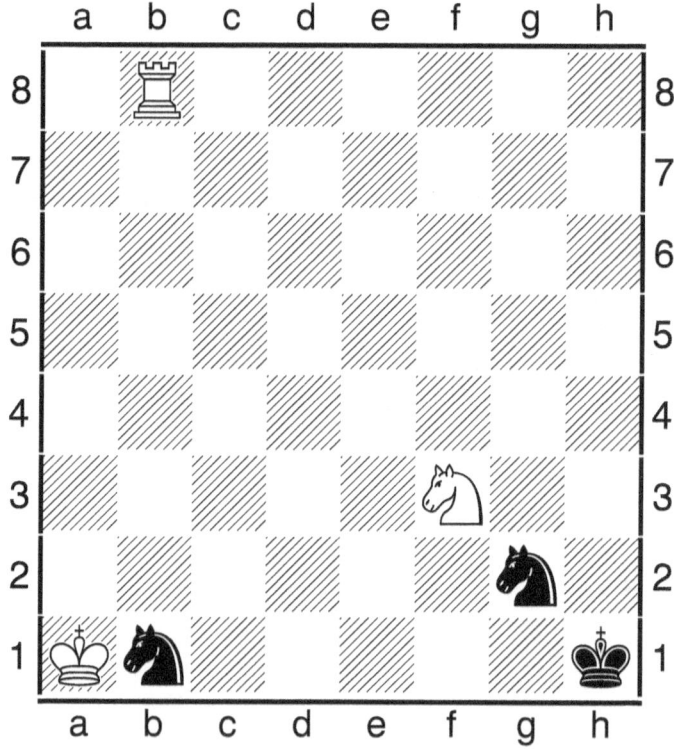

KRN vs knn
White is ahead by two pawn units but can you find the best way
to proceed here?

Computer-Generated Chess Problem 01108

White to Play and Mate in 5
Chesthetica v10.17 (Selangor, Malaysia)
Generated on 13 Jul 2016 at 10:52:47 AM
Solvability Estimate = Difficult

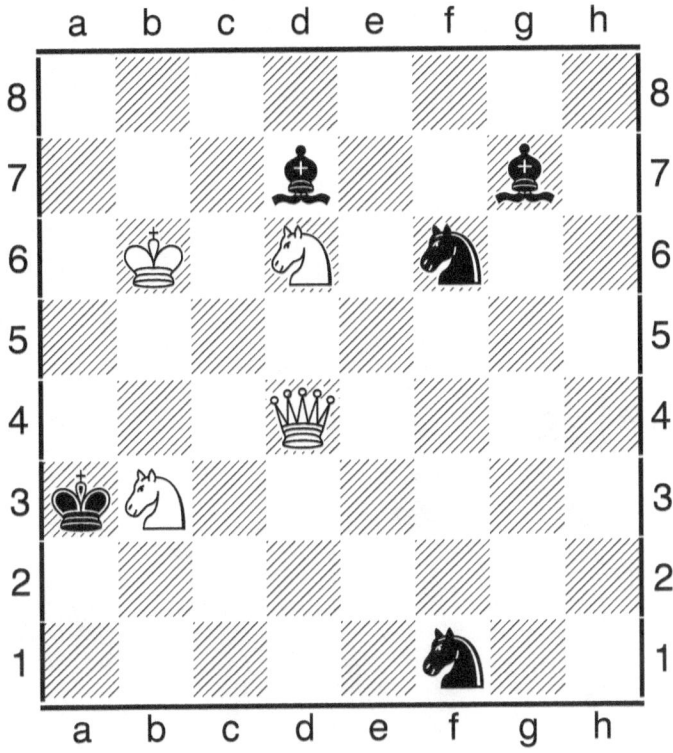

KQNN vs kbbnn
White is ahead by three pawn units (one minor piece's worth) but
can you find the best way to proceed here?

Computer-Generated Chess Problem 01126

White to Play and Mate in 5
Chesthetica v10.18 (Selangor, Malaysia)
Generated on 1 Aug 2016 at 12:49:06 AM
Solvability Estimate = Difficult

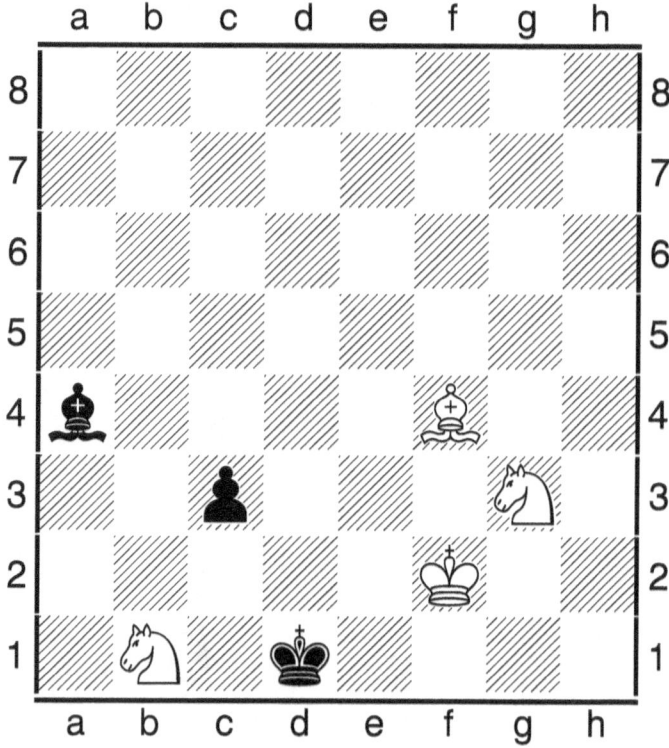

KBNN vs kbp
White is ahead by five pawn units (a rook's worth) but can you
find the best way to proceed here?

Computer-Generated Chess Problem 01130

White to Play and Mate in 4
Chesthetica v10.19 (Selangor, Malaysia)
Generated on 1 Aug 2016 at 3:35:29 PM
Solvability Estimate = Easy

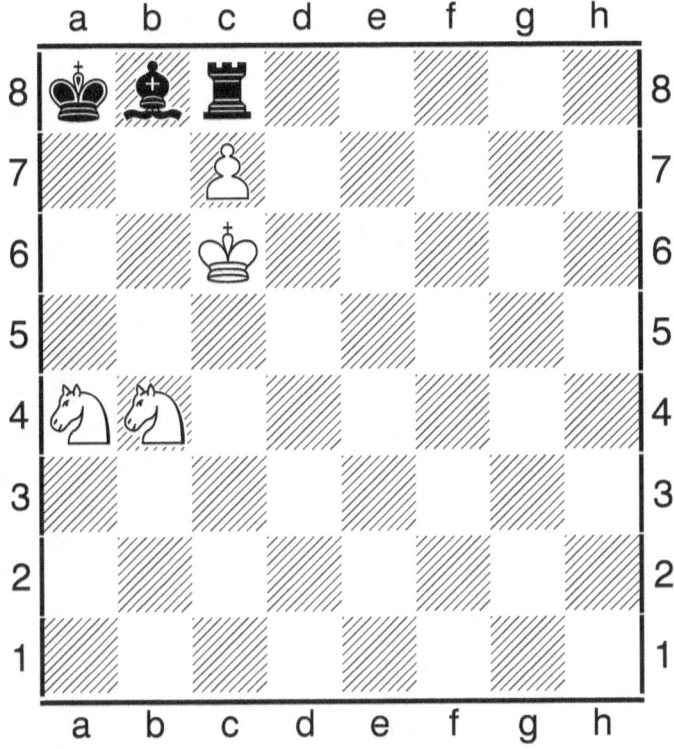

KNNP vs krb
White is actually down by one pawn unit. White is also close to a
pawn promotion.

Computer-Generated Chess Problem 01147

White to Play and Mate in 4
Chesthetica v10.18 (Selangor, Malaysia)
Generated on 20 Aug 2016 at 6:34:44 PM
Solvability Estimate = Moderate

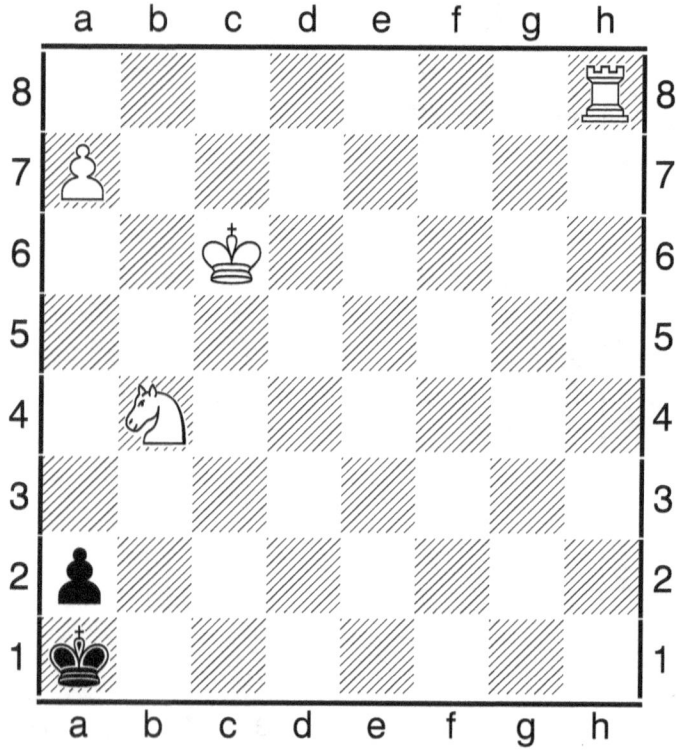

KRNP vs kp
White is ahead by eight pawn units but can you find the best way
to proceed here? White is also close to a pawn promotion but so
is Black.

Computer-Generated Chess Problem 01155

White to Play and Mate in 5
Chesthetica v10.20 (Selangor, Malaysia)
Generated on 26 Aug 2016 at 12:30:36 AM
Solvability Estimate = Moderate

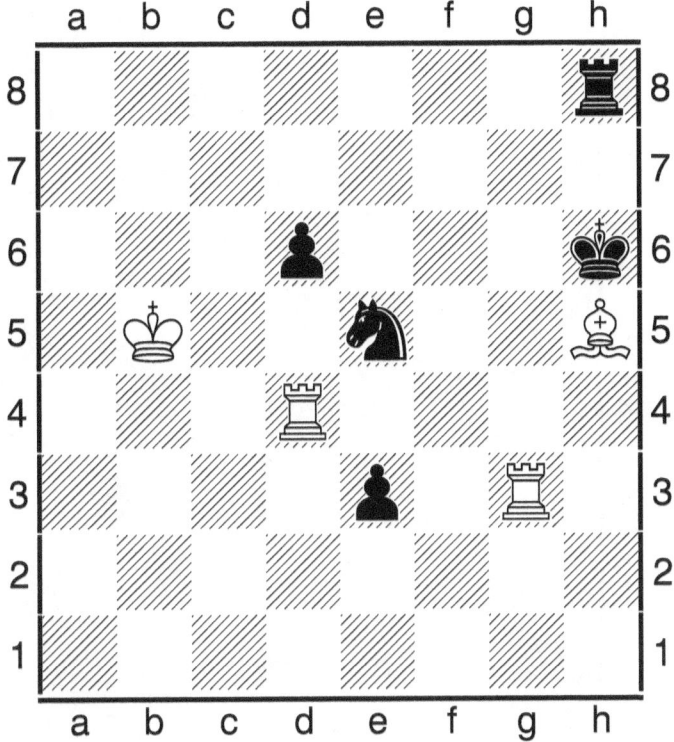

KRRB vs krnpp
White is ahead by three pawn units (one minor piece's worth) but can you find the best way to proceed here?

Computer-Generated Chess Problem 01157

White to Play and Mate in 3
Chesthetica v10.20 (Selangor, Malaysia)
Generated on 27 Aug 2016 at 1:24:04 AM
Solvability Estimate = Moderate

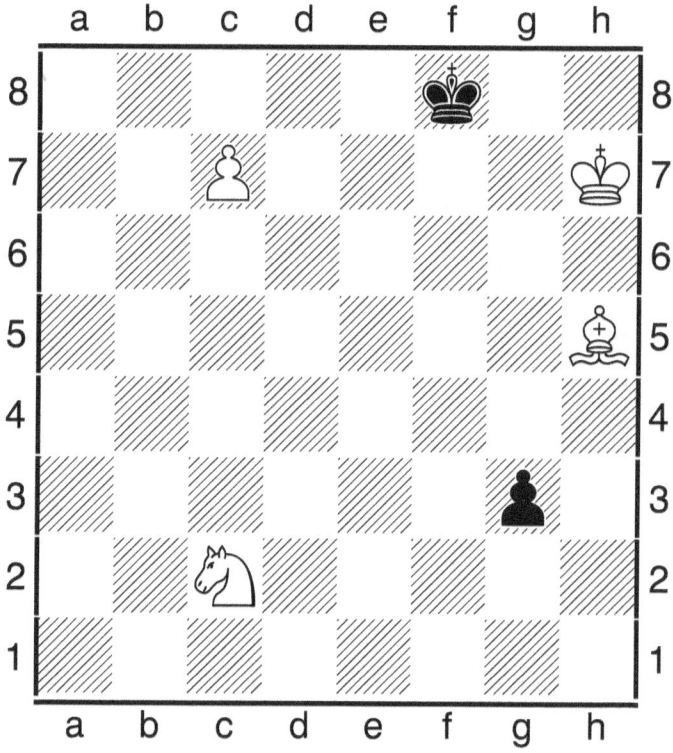

KBNP vs kp
White is ahead by six pawn units (two minor piece's worth) but
can you find the best way to proceed here? White is also close to
a pawn promotion.

Chapter 2

Selected Compositions Generated Between September and November 2016

There is a virtually infinite number of legal positions in chess, or around 10^{46}, to be more specific. Even to this day, nobody really knows what the precise number is or how to calculate it. If there were 500 *billion* Earths, there would be more legal chess positions than the atoms that made up all the sand on all those Earths. What does this mean, really? It means that for all the games that humanity (including all its chess engines) has played and for all the chess problems that have been composed until now and likely for the rest of our future existence, we would barely even have scratched the surface of the game.

People are still amazed at interesting games and swashbuckling sacrifices. You may have noticed that these things often make the chess news circuit. Articles are written about them when they happen, especially between grandmasters in tournaments. Articles are also written about amazing compositions. People still talk and write about things like these decades and even centuries after they occurred. That is how valuable some positions and move sequences can be. How many of these, do you think, remain to be discovered given the number of legal positions in chess? What percentage has already been discovered or even imagined?

The answer here is simple. Again, we have barely scratched the surface. The legendary grandmaster and eighth World Chess Champion, Mikhail Tal is reputed to have said, *"Every game is like a poem, valuable and unique in its own right.*" I tend to agree with him. You might think that games between amateurs have no or little value and you may be right but beauty is generally in the eye of the beholder. Amateurs may be equally impressed by certain things in chess as grandmasters are impressed by other things in chess. They are on different levels, for sure, but it does not mean either necessarily enjoys the game less or more than the other. This is one of the things that drove me to develop *Chesthetica*, or more importantly, take it from being just a kind of automatic evaluator of chess problems to a bona fide composer of chess problems.

The distinction here may not be obvious to most but consider how being a renowned or master art critic does not at all somehow make one a master artist. There is a vast chasm between mere evaluation and the *creation* of something original that has some value. What *Chesthetica* does, for instance, is something even *AlphaZero* does not (or cannot) do using its machine learning approach. Perhaps Google has not bothered to even try because the emphasis in artificial intelligence (AI) has largely been on beating the World Champion or *playing* chess better. Chess problem composition, however, is far more subjective but far more demanding, or at least more interesting, from an AI perspective.

In any case, this second chapter is fairly short. The shortest, in fact. This is because there was incidentally an unusually large number of selected compositions generated just in December 2016 that a whole chapter could be devoted to it alone, i.e. chapter 3. I am not sure or have forgotten the reason for this 'Cambrian explosion' at that time. Then again, it has been impossible for me to ever predict the quantity of compositions any instance of *Chesthetica* will create in a given period, much less what those compositions will look like. This second chapter features only mates in 4 and 5. If you skipped the first chapter and are interested only in these 'longer mates', you are in the right place.

Computer-Generated Chess Problem 01170

White to Play and Mate in 4
Chesthetica v10.21 (Selangor, Malaysia)
Generated on 3 Sep 2016 at 12:56:08 PM
Solvability Estimate = Difficult

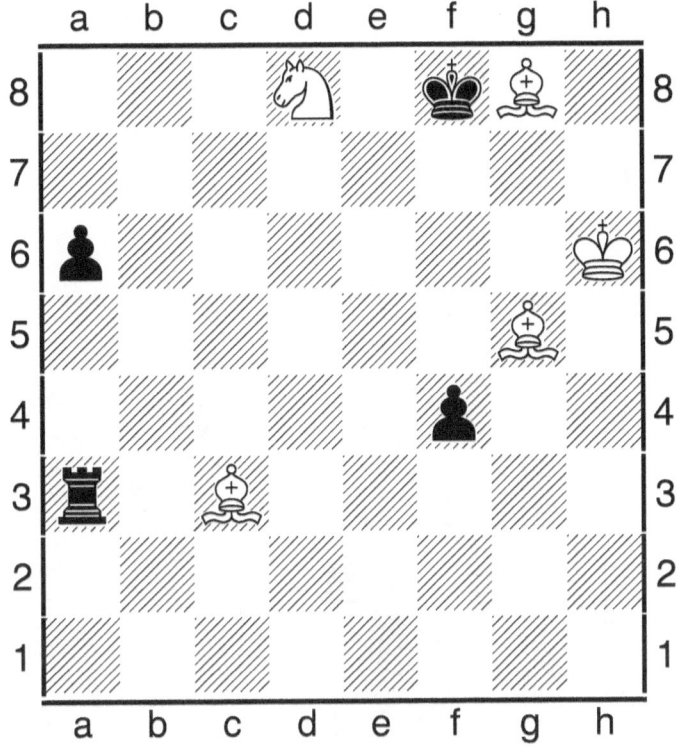

KBBBN vs krpp
White is ahead by five pawn units (a rook's worth) but can you
find the best way to proceed here?

Computer-Generated Chess Problem 01173

White to Play and Mate in 5
Chesthetica v10.21 (Selangor, Malaysia)
Generated on 4 Sep 2016 at 7:57:22 AM
Solvability Estimate = Easy

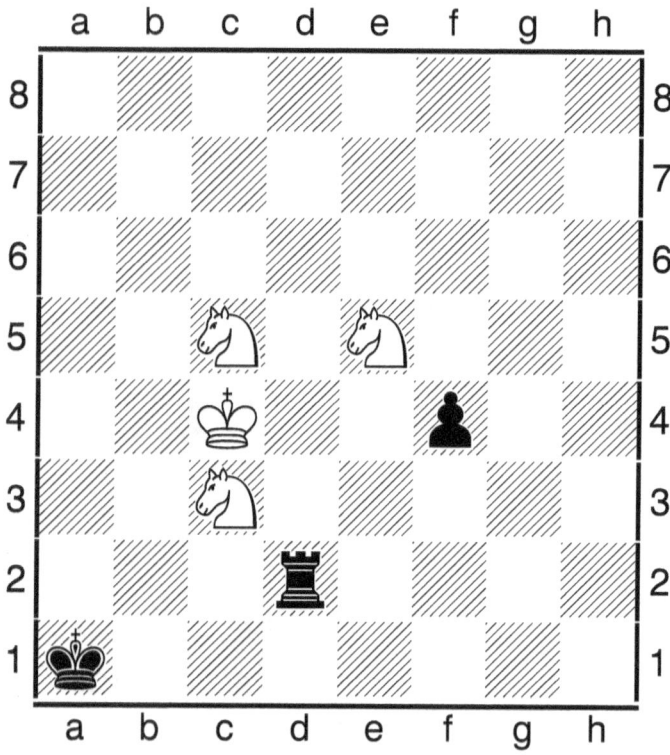

KNNN vs krp
White is ahead by three pawn units (one minor piece's worth) but
can you find the best way to proceed here?

Computer-Generated Chess Problem 01204

White to Play and Mate in 5
Chesthetica v10.28 (Selangor, Malaysia)
Generated on 7 Oct 2016 at 5:22:03 AM
Solvability Estimate = Difficult

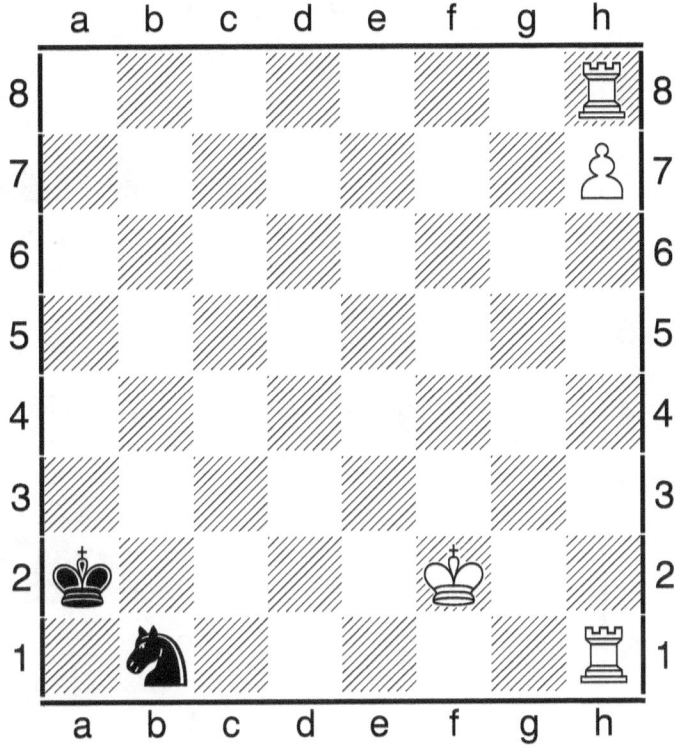

KRRP vs kn
White is ahead by eight pawn units but can you find the best way
to proceed here? White is also close to a pawn promotion.

Computer-Generated Chess Problem 01218

White to Play and Mate in 5
Chesthetica v10.28 (Selangor, Malaysia)
Generated on 12 Oct 2016 at 9:38:12 PM
Solvability Estimate = Difficult

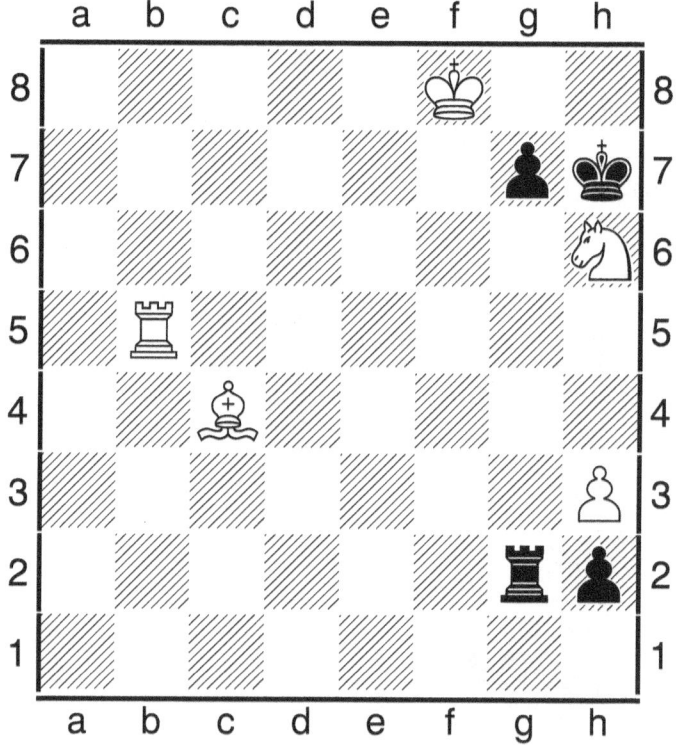

KRBNP vs krpp
White is ahead by five pawn units (a rook's worth) but can you
find the best way to proceed here? Black is also close to a pawn
promotion.

Computer-Generated Chess Problem 01221

White to Play and Mate in 4
Chesthetica v10.28 (Selangor, Malaysia)
Generated on 13 Oct 2016 at 3:44:12 PM
Solvability Estimate = Difficult

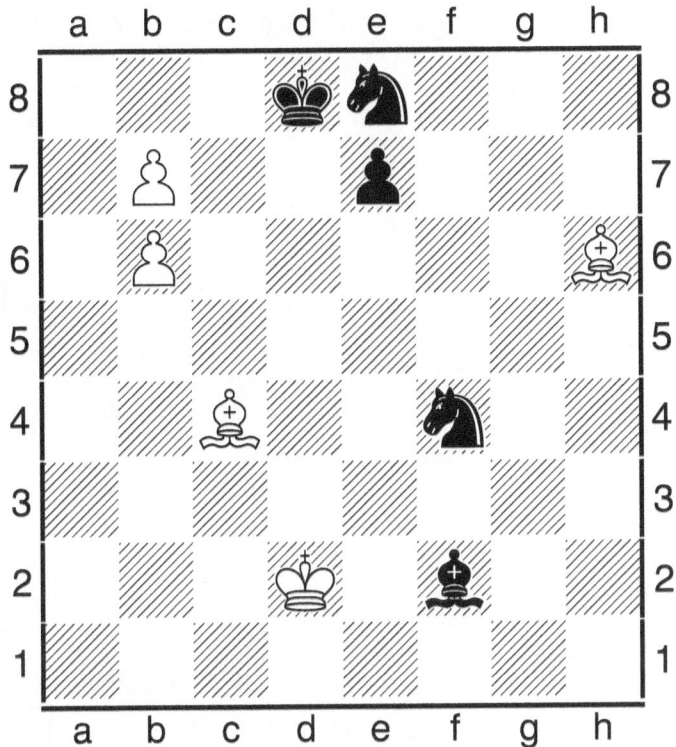

KBBPP vs kbnnp
White is actually down by two pawn units. White is also close to a
pawn promotion.

Computer-Generated Chess Problem 01224

White to Play and Mate in 5
Chesthetica v10.28 (Selangor, Malaysia)
Generated on 14 Oct 2016 at 9:46:56 AM
Solvability Estimate = Moderate

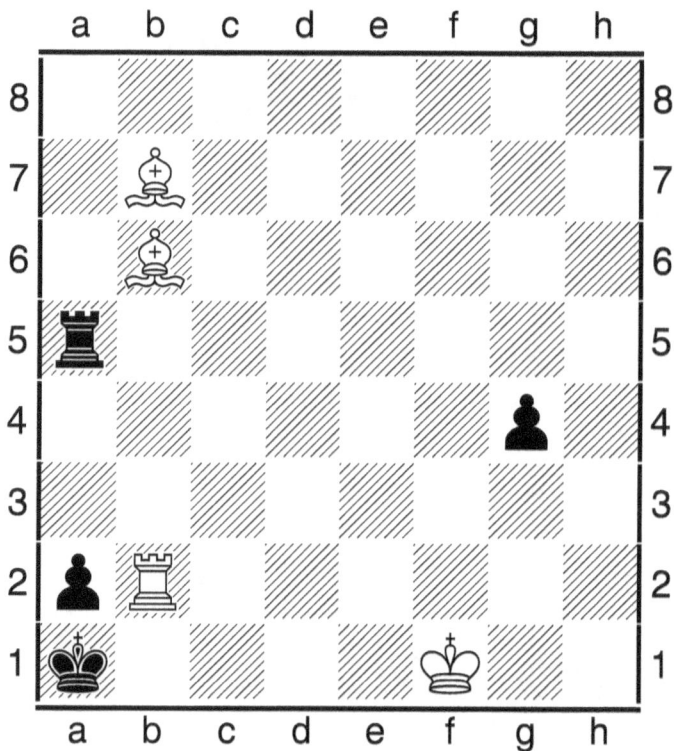

KRBB vs krpp
White is ahead by four pawn units but can you find the best way
to proceed here? Black is also close to a pawn promotion.

Computer-Generated Chess Problem 01268

White to Play and Mate in 5
Chesthetica v10.28 (Selangor, Malaysia)
Generated on 26 Nov 2016 at 12:34:38 PM
Solvability Estimate = Difficult

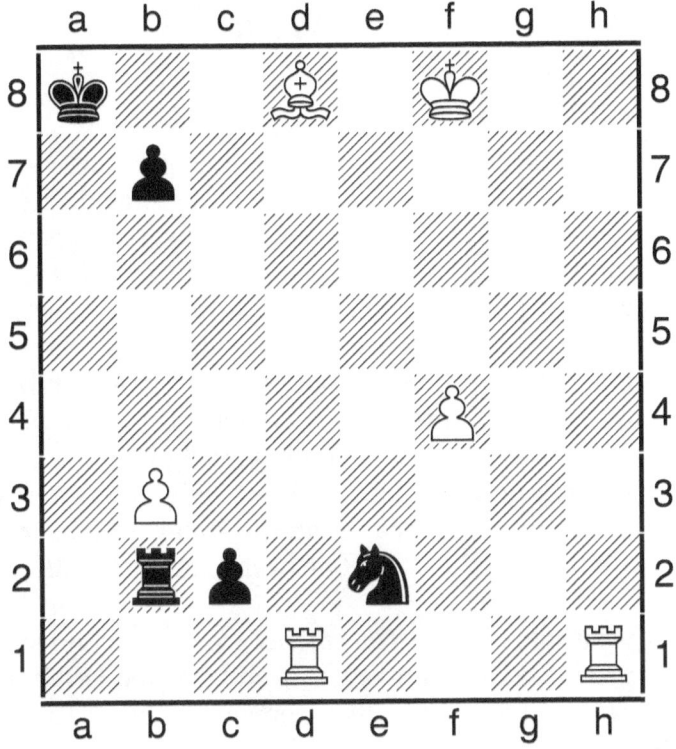

KRRBPP vs krnpp
White is ahead by five pawn units (a rook's worth) but can you find the best way to proceed here? Black is also close to a pawn promotion.

Chapter 3

Selected Compositions Generated in December 2016

There was a chapter like this in the previous volume as well, i.e. a whole chapter devoted to compositions generated in just a single month. As before, it was not planned but just so happened to be the case. Even more intriguing, as I just confirmed this myself, there has been exactly one chapter like this in every volume since the first one. Imagine that. None of it planned. What are the odds of such a thing happening? Rare, but not nearly impossible. Similarly, could it be that *Chesthetica's* compositions are generated by random chance? If someone merely tossed pieces randomly on the chessboard (assuming each landed nicely in a square), would compositions like you see in these volumes appear again and again? Not likely is the correct answer. Extremely unlikely, in fact.

This is what makes what *Chesthetica* does so interesting to many. Even more interesting, arguably, is whether the DSNS technology it uses can be applied to other domains where creativity plays a significant role. We may never know the answer to this unless there is enough interest and drive in testing it in other domains. Unfortunately, this requires considerable investment in terms of resources and time, never mind the expertise. Even deep learning has its roots stretching back over 60 years so it may be premature to talk about the DSNS as if it was already on the same level as deep learning today, never mind having the vast resources of a major corporation like IBM or Google behind it as well.

The point here being that while the DSNS certainly seems to work quite well in the domain of chess composition, its true potential may remain untapped for decades, perhaps centuries, to come. I try to do what I can as a typical academic in a developing country (or 'emerging economy' as the euphemism today goes) but without the necessary interest and backing to take it further (e.g. into more serious domains), even my ability to function as a primary consultant on the DSNS remains 'untapped'. Nevertheless, I hope I have written enough about it, and in sufficient detail, given my publications, that anyone sufficiently interested in taking it further will have the essential means of doing so, even very far into the future.

Just the possibility that it could lead to something more than it is now make those efforts worthwhile. One really has to wonder, then, what wonders of technology might still remain hidden or having never seen the light of day among the millions of publications, academic or otherwise, produced by mankind thus far? Will a major breakthrough in AI be the result of some interested party stumbling across an idea or even a meticulously-described approach written some 50 or 100 years earlier by a nonentity? That would be somewhat embarrassing, I suppose, but less so than if it remained undiscovered, or even worse, lost for good somehow; due to a fire, or even a corrupted hard drive as the case may be. Alas, that has been and often still is the state of humanity's crawl toward useful knowledge acquisition.

This third chapter includes a collection of forced mates (3, 4 and 5 moves). White also happens to always be significantly ahead in material. Incidentally, there happens to be an equal number of compositions here deemed 'moderate' and 'difficult' by my 'solvability estimate' algorithm (this was first introduced in volume 3). Is this what one might expect given that White is always significantly ahead in material? You be the judge. You may even find, given your personal experience, that some are actually 'easy'. Solvability, if I may be the first to use this term in the context of chess, may not be in the eye of the beholder per se but is relative to the experience of him or her nonetheless.

Computer-Generated Chess Problem 01277

White to Play and Mate in 4
Chesthetica v10.28 (Selangor, Malaysia)
Generated on 1 Dec 2016 at 5:46:29 AM
Solvability Estimate = Moderate

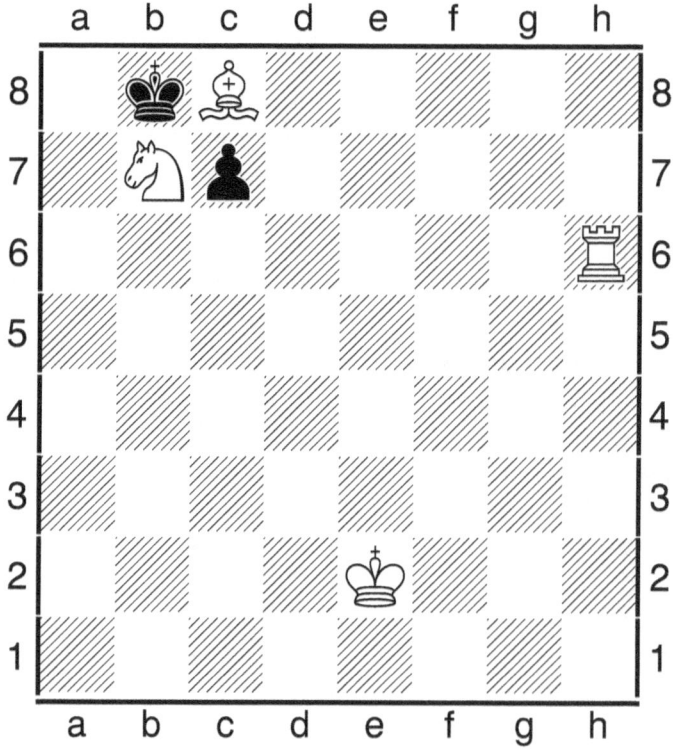

KRBN vs kp
White is ahead by 10 pawn units (two rook's worth) but can you
find the best way to proceed here?

Computer-Generated Chess Problem 01279

White to Play and Mate in 4
Chesthetica v10.28 (Selangor, Malaysia)
Generated on 3 Dec 2016 at 5:55:52 AM
Solvability Estimate = Moderate

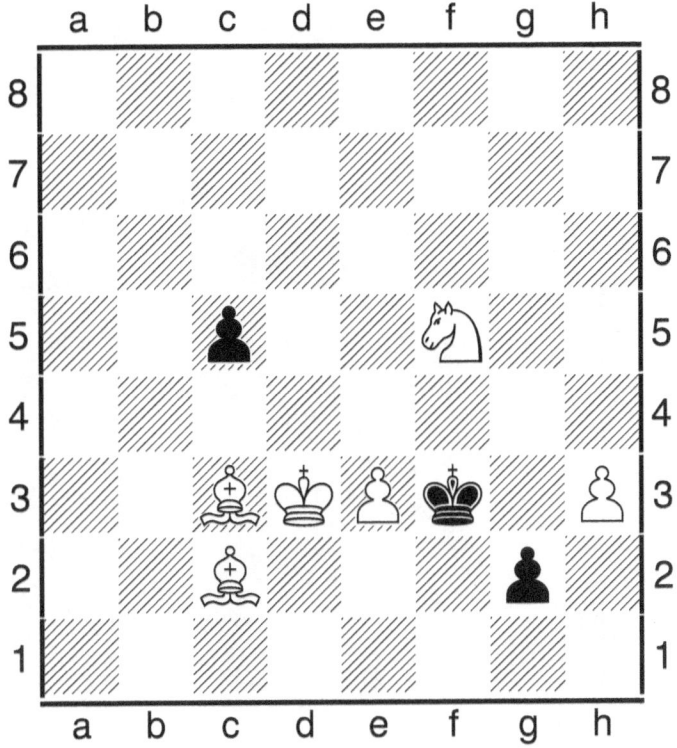

KBBNPP vs kpp
White is ahead by nine pawn units (a queen's worth) but can you find the best way to proceed here? Black is also close to a pawn promotion.

Computer-Generated Chess Problem 01285

White to Play and Mate in 3
Chesthetica v10.28 (Selangor, Malaysia)
Generated on 6 Dec 2016 at 4:29:15 PM
Solvability Estimate = Moderate

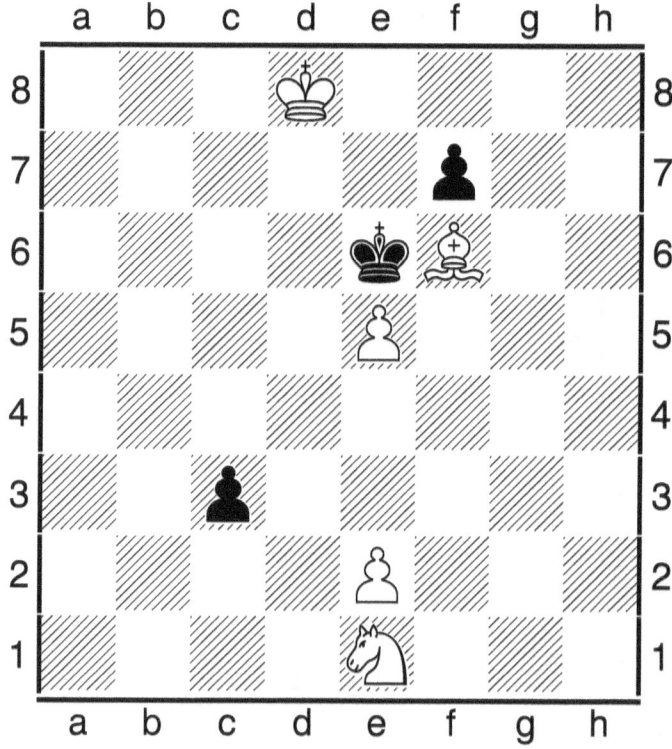

KBNPP vs kpp
White is ahead by six pawn units (two minor piece's worth) but
can you find the best way to proceed here?

Computer-Generated Chess Problem 01289

White to Play and Mate in 3
Chesthetica v10.28 (Selangor, Malaysia)
Generated on 9 Dec 2016 at 3:38:30 AM
Solvability Estimate = Difficult

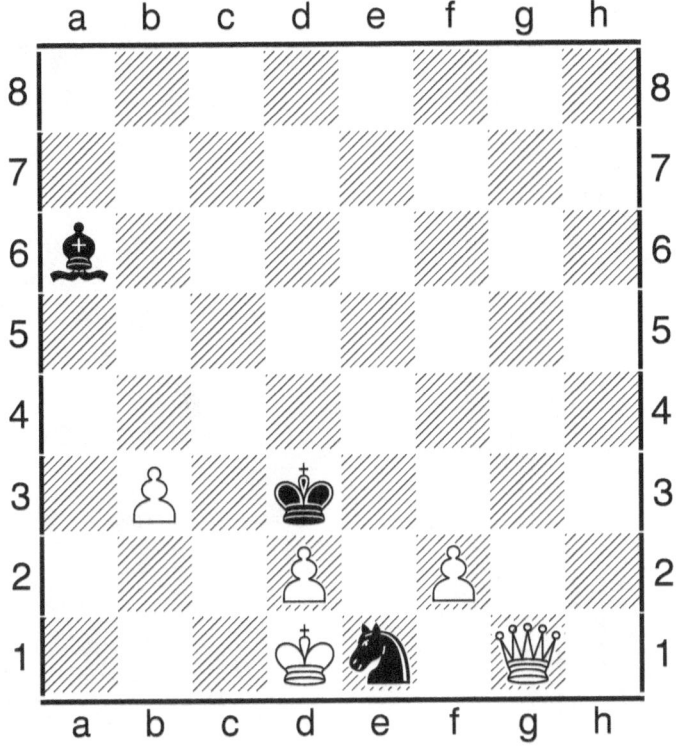

KQPPP vs kbn
White is ahead by six pawn units (two minor piece's worth) but
can you find the best way to proceed here?

Computer-Generated Chess Problem 01297

White to Play and Mate in 3
Chesthetica v10.28 (Selangor, Malaysia)
Generated on 10 Dec 2016 at 1:24:26 AM
Solvability Estimate = Moderate

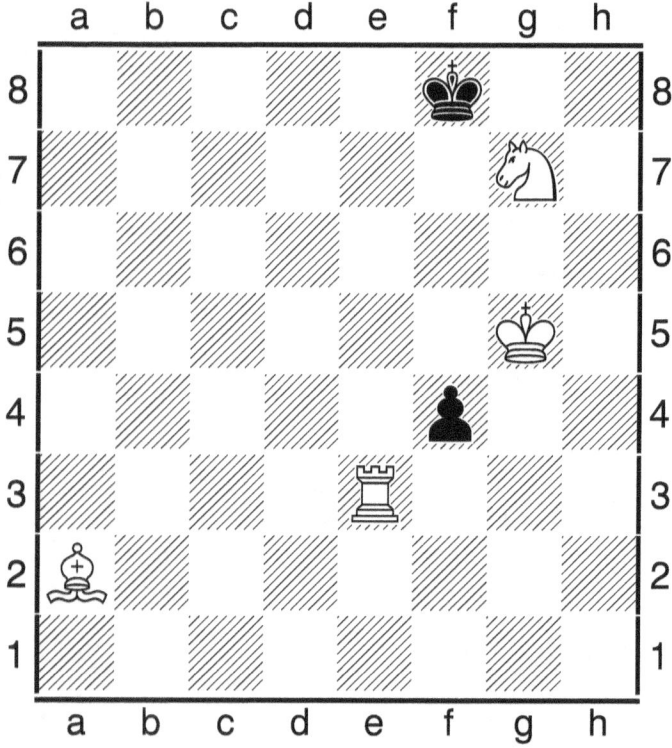

KRBN vs kp
White is ahead by 10 pawn units (two rook's worth) but can you find the best way to proceed here?

Computer-Generated Chess Problem 01300

White to Play and Mate in 5
Chesthetica v10.28 (Selangor, Malaysia)
Generated on 10 Dec 2016 at 8:01:55 AM
Solvability Estimate = Difficult

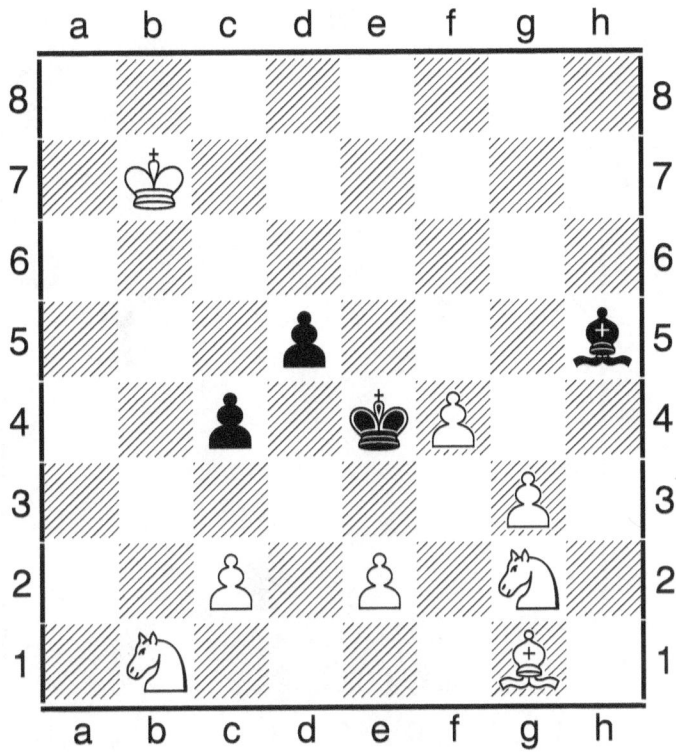

KBNNPPPP vs kbpp
White is ahead by eight pawn units but can you find the best way
to proceed here?

Computer-Generated Chess Problem 01307

White to Play and Mate in 4
Chesthetica v10.31 (Selangor, Malaysia)
Generated on 11 Dec 2016 at 1:25:25 PM
Solvability Estimate = Difficult

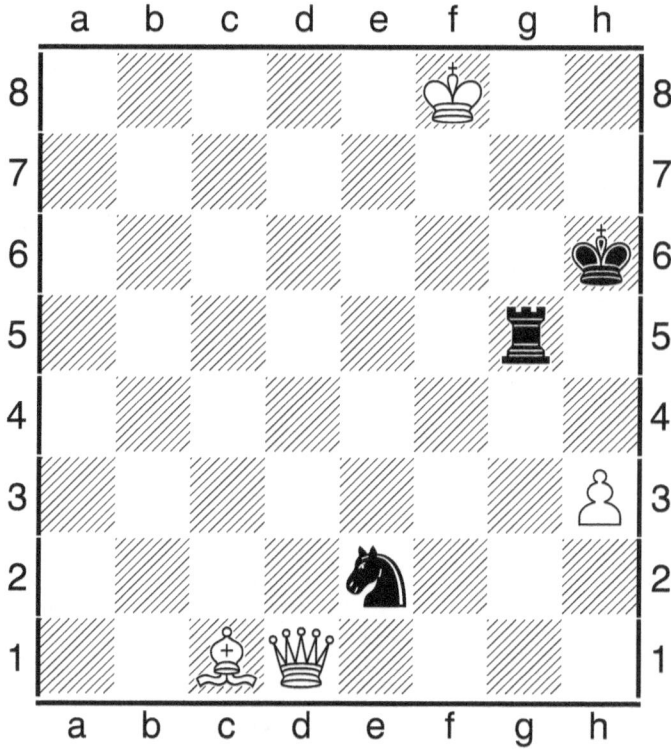

KQBP vs krn
White is ahead by five pawn units (a rook's worth) but can you
find the best way to proceed here?

Computer-Generated Chess Problem 01309

White to Play and Mate in 4
Chesthetica v10.31 (Selangor, Malaysia)
Generated on 13 Dec 2016 at 1:50:29 AM
Solvability Estimate = Difficult

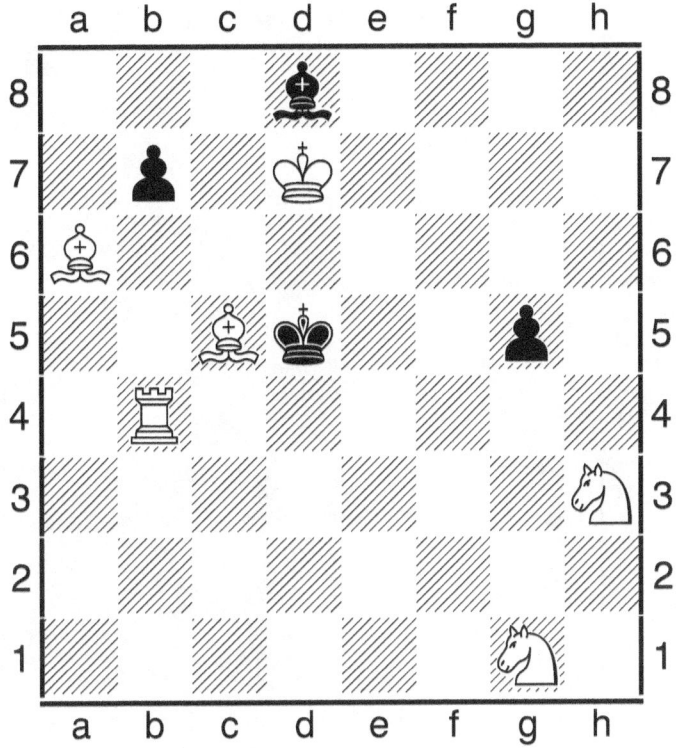

KRBBNN vs kbpp
White is ahead by 12 pawn units (four minor piece's worth) but
can you find the best way to proceed here?

Computer-Generated Chess Problem 01314

White to Play and Mate in 5
Chesthetica v10.31 (Selangor, Malaysia)
Generated on 15 Dec 2016 at 7:52:18 AM
Solvability Estimate = Difficult

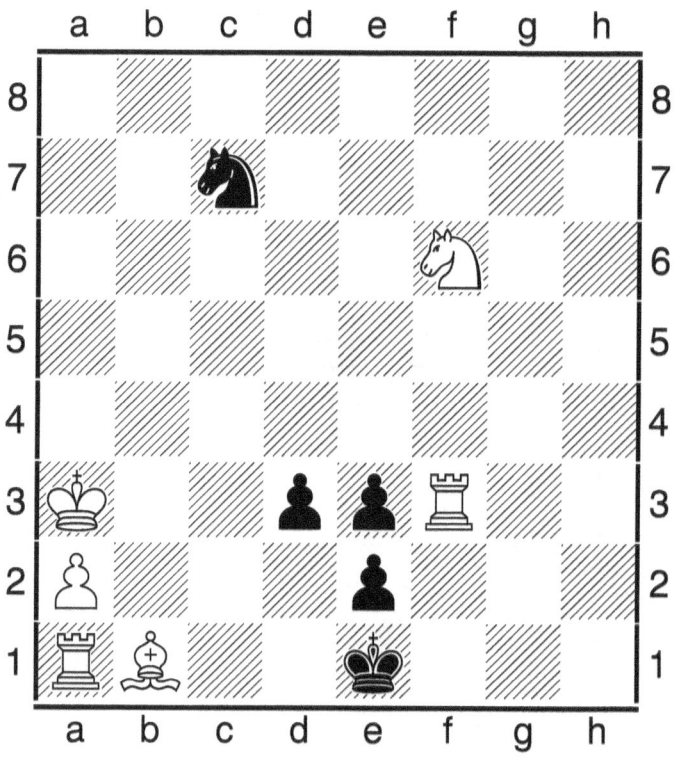

KRRBNP vs knppp
White is ahead by 11 pawn units but can you find the best way to
proceed here? Black is also close to a pawn promotion.

Computer-Generated Chess Problem 01326

White to Play and Mate in 4
Chesthetica v10.31 (Selangor, Malaysia)
Generated on 22 Dec 2016 at 10:12:34 AM
Solvability Estimate = Moderate

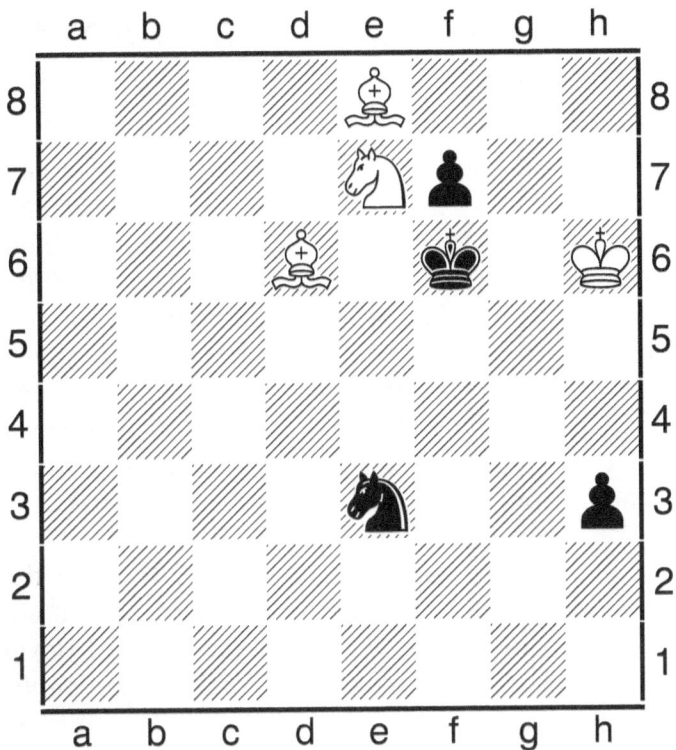

KBBN vs knpp
White is ahead by four pawn units but can you find the best way
to proceed here?

Chapter 4

Selected Compositions Generated Between January and May 2017

So we enter the year 2017 now. You may be wondering what *Chesthetica* has composed in the year 2020 or later, depending on when you are reading this. Chances are, the more recent compositions are available online (just google them) and the ones even more recent than that are either unreleased or still being collected for online publication at some point in the near future. The first few compositions by Chesthetica were generated way back in 2010. Specifically, the first 16 and between July and November 2010. These were composed using an older 'experience table' computational approach and limited to forced three-movers.

I wrote an academic paper about this in 2011 (see the reference section at the end of the book). The ones composed using the DSNS computational creativity approach which I developed later were first generated in August 2014. I only started publishing them online (including the ones from 2010) in December 2014 on the Chesthetica YouTube channel. So there has always been and remains a gap between the time a composition is generated and when it is made public online; albeit a narrowing gap now that the process is more established and smoother. Longer mates (4 and 5 moves) were introduced only in June 2015. Study-like constructs in August of the same year.

The coding or development process of *Chesthetica* over the years has been a whole other (both challenging and satisfying) experience. My focus was initially to computationally evaluate chess problems aesthetically. This was a milestone in itself and being able to demonstrate that experimentally earned me my PhD. It was only after that that I decided to pursue the perhaps even more lofty idea of a computer program actually composing original chess problems, aesthetically-pleasing or otherwise, but preferably so. This too, to my knowledge, had never been done before in a fully-autonomous way. The typical approach to 'automatic' composition had been to search using computer heuristics for interesting-looking endgame positions in large endgame databases (or 'tablebases' as they are sometimes called).

The largest to date is still the 'Lomonosov 7-man' collection calculated on a supercomputer of the same name in Moscow back in 2012. If a computer was used to search for interesting mate combinations using this resource, despite having over 500 trillion unique positions, they would still be limited to 7 pieces, at most. *Chesthetica's* compositions, as you can already see, have no such limitations and therefore could not have been sourced from such a place. Hence the novelty of the DSNS computational creativity approach. Besides, the number of possible positions increases in a somewhat exponential manner so we are unlikely to see exhaustive collections involving ever more pieces any time soon, if ever.

Even if we do have 8, 9 or 10-piece tablebases some day, finding interesting or aesthetically-pleasing sequences in them would be like looking for a needle in a haystack, even using a computer. So you may begin to now see why the approach Chesthetica uses is perhaps a better one in this regard. To have a computer, using artificial intelligence (or more specifically, computational creativity), to actually compose original chess problems from scratch and then have humans decide which ones they like. This is far less unlike how human composers compose problems, you would have to agree. Anyway, chapter 4 has 17 compositions of the mate in 3, 4 and 5 varieties. If you have gone through the previous chapters, you will find more of the same here.

Computer-Generated Chess Problem 01356

White to Play and Mate in 3
Chesthetica v10.31 (Selangor, Malaysia)
Generated on 13 Jan 2017 at 7:13:21 AM
Solvability Estimate = Difficult

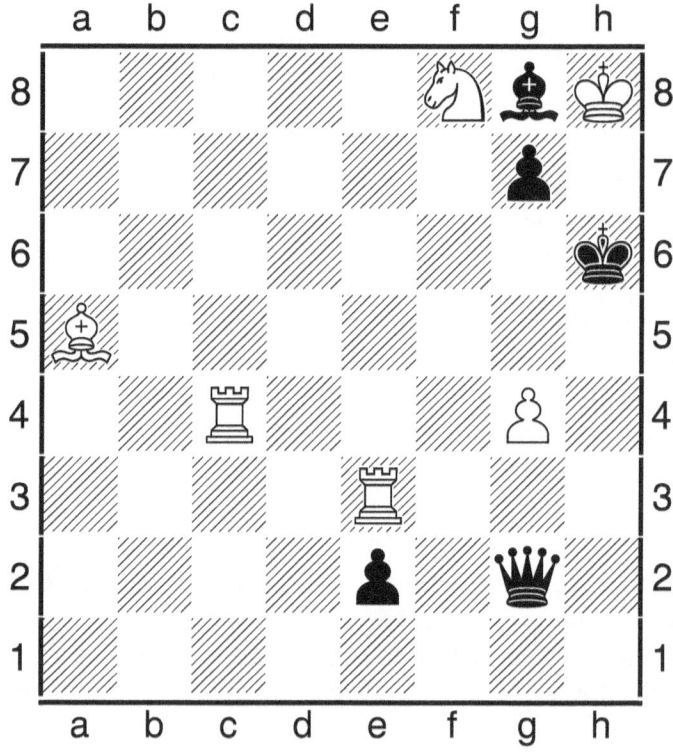

KRRBNP vs kqbpp
White is ahead by three pawn units (one minor piece's worth) but can you find the best way to proceed here? Black is also close to a pawn promotion.

Computer-Generated Chess Problem 01366

White to Play and Mate in 4
Chesthetica v10.31 (Selangor, Malaysia)
Generated on 19 Jan 2017 at 4:39:08 AM
Solvability Estimate = Moderate

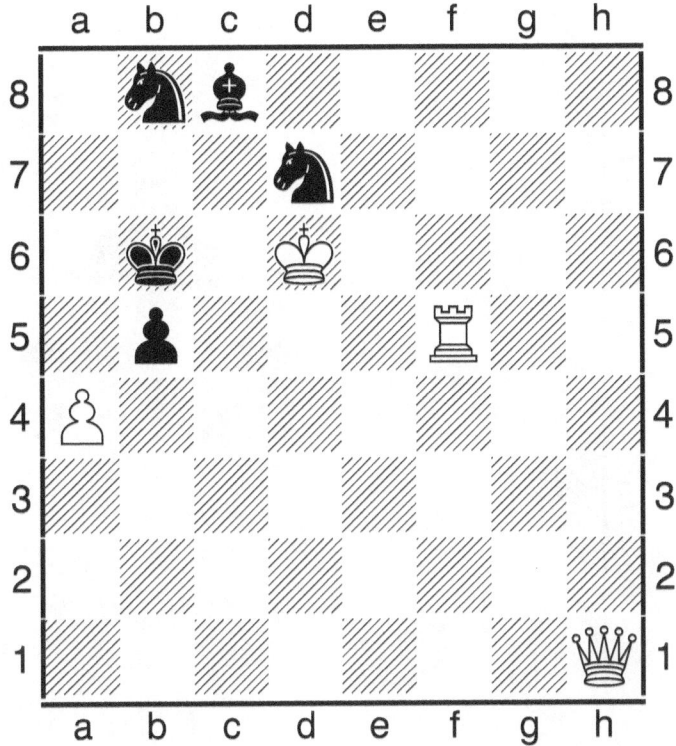

KQRP vs kbnnp
White is ahead by five pawn units (a rook's worth) but can you
find the best way to proceed here?

Computer-Generated Chess Problem 01372

White to Play and Mate in 3
Chesthetica v10.31 (Selangor, Malaysia)
Generated on 21 Jan 2017 at 11:46:44 AM
Solvability Estimate = Difficult

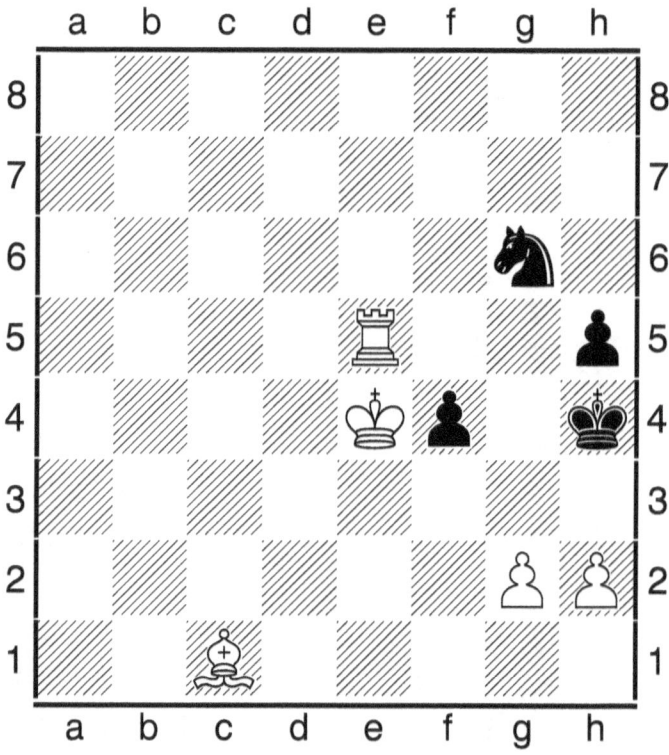

KRBPP vs knpp
White is ahead by five pawn units (a rook's worth) but can you
find the best way to proceed here?

Computer-Generated Chess Problem 01406

White to Play and Mate in 3
Chesthetica v10.31 (Selangor, Malaysia)
Generated on 11 Feb 2017 at 1:06:37 PM
Solvability Estimate = Difficult

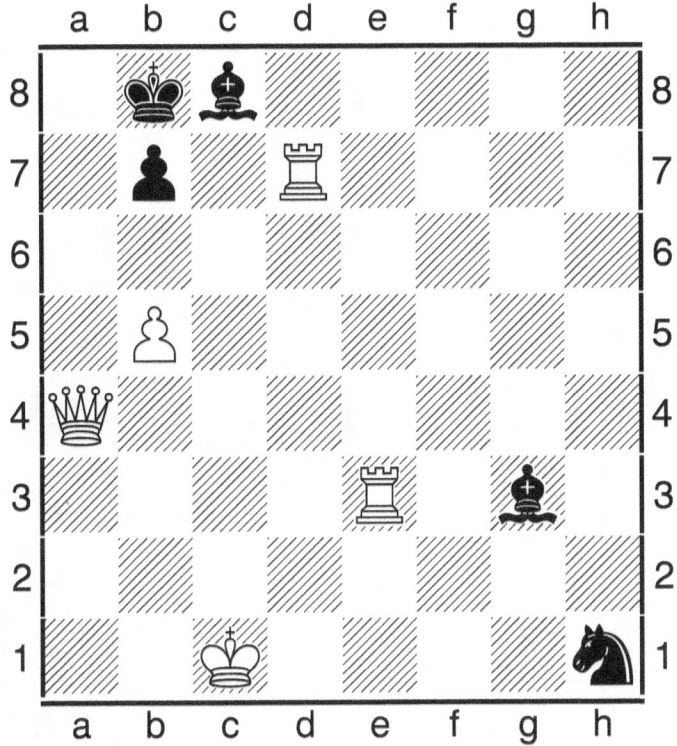

KQRRP vs kbbnp
White is ahead by 10 pawn units (two rook's worth) but can you
find the best way to proceed here?

Computer-Generated Chess Problem 01414

White to Play and Mate in 5
Chesthetica v10.33 (Selangor, Malaysia)
Generated on 18 Feb 2017 at 12:53:00 PM
Solvability Estimate = Difficult

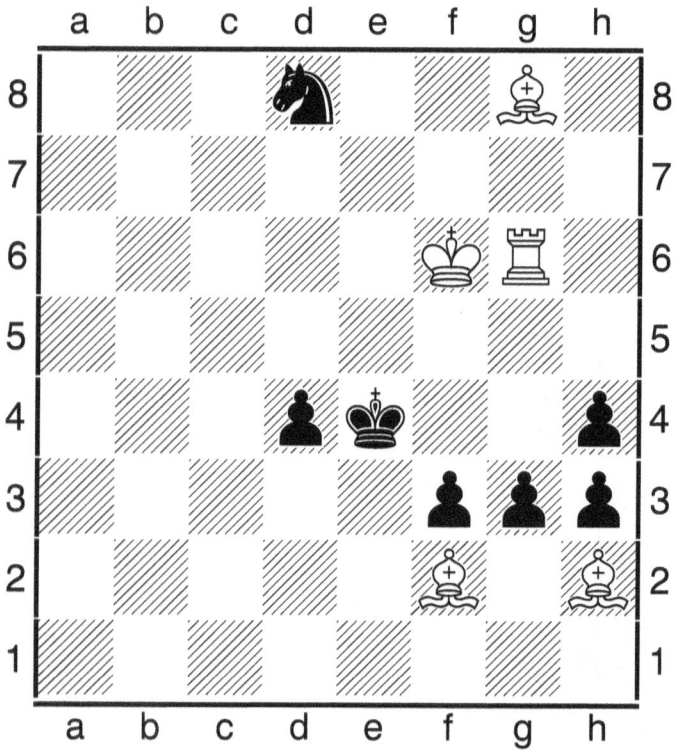

KRBBB vs knppppp
White is ahead by six pawn units (two minor piece's worth) but
can you find the best way to proceed here?

Computer-Generated Chess Problem 01419

White to Play and Mate in 3
Chesthetica v10.33 (Selangor, Malaysia)
Generated on 20 Feb 2017 at 12:55:19 PM
Solvability Estimate = Difficult

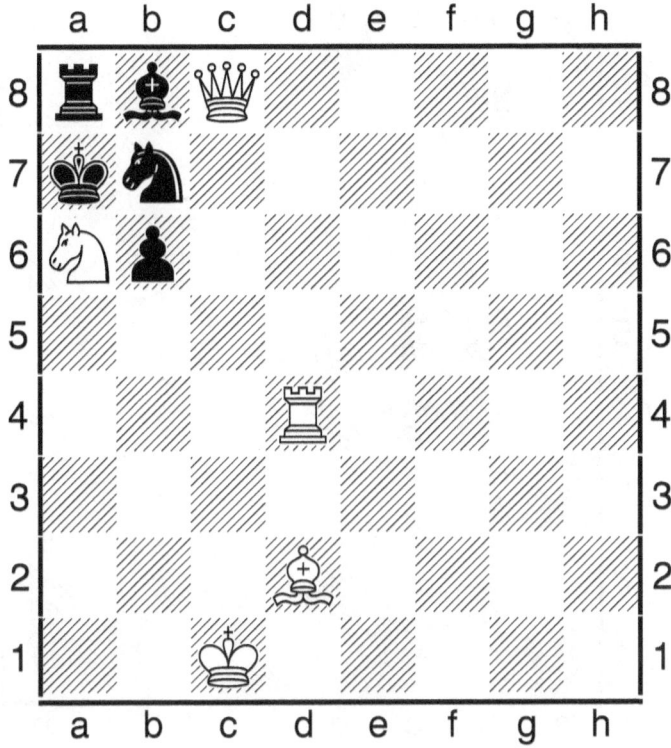

KQRBN vs krbnp
White is ahead by eight pawn units but can you find the best way to proceed here?

Computer-Generated Chess Problem 01429

White to Play and Mate in 3
Chesthetica v10.33 (Selangor, Malaysia)
Generated on 3 Mar 2017 at 9:20:49 AM
Solvability Estimate = Difficult

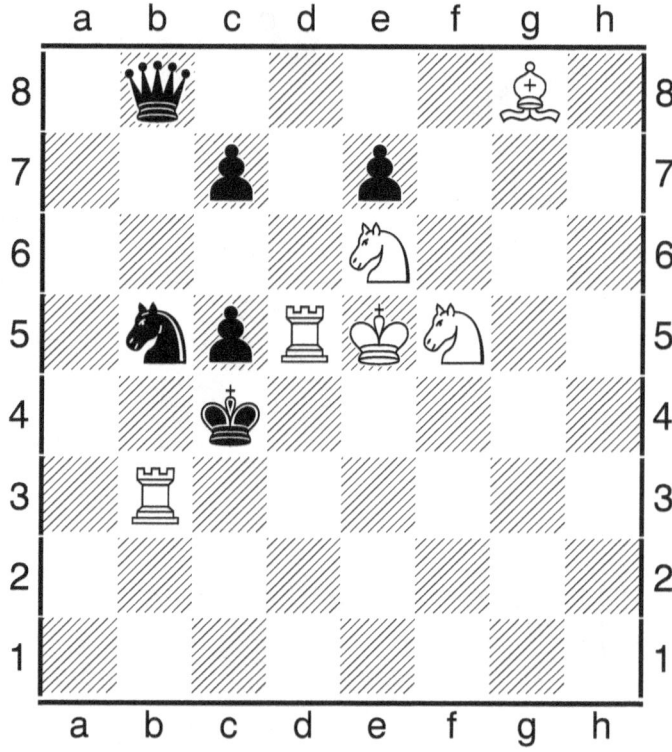

KRRBNN vs kqnppp
White is ahead by four pawn units but can you find the best way
to proceed here?

Computer-Generated Chess Problem 01446

White to Play and Mate in 3
Chesthetica v10.34 (Selangor, Malaysia)
Generated on 21 Mar 2017 at 11:29:25 PM
Solvability Estimate = Difficult

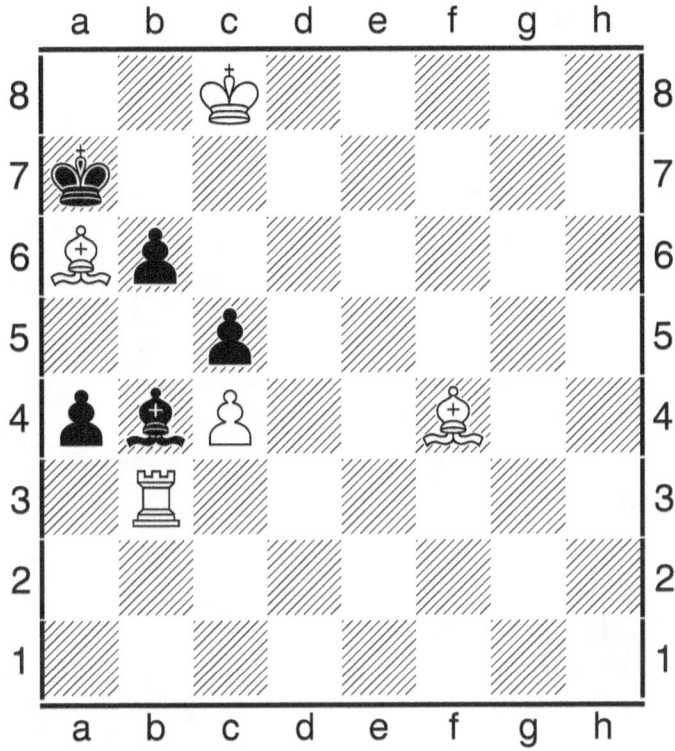

KRBBP vs kbppp
White is ahead by six pawn units (two minor piece's worth) but
can you find the best way to proceed here?

Computer-Generated Chess Problem 01455

White to Play and Mate in 4
Chesthetica v10.34 (Selangor, Malaysia)
Generated on 2 Apr 2017 at 2:15:10 AM
Solvability Estimate = Moderate

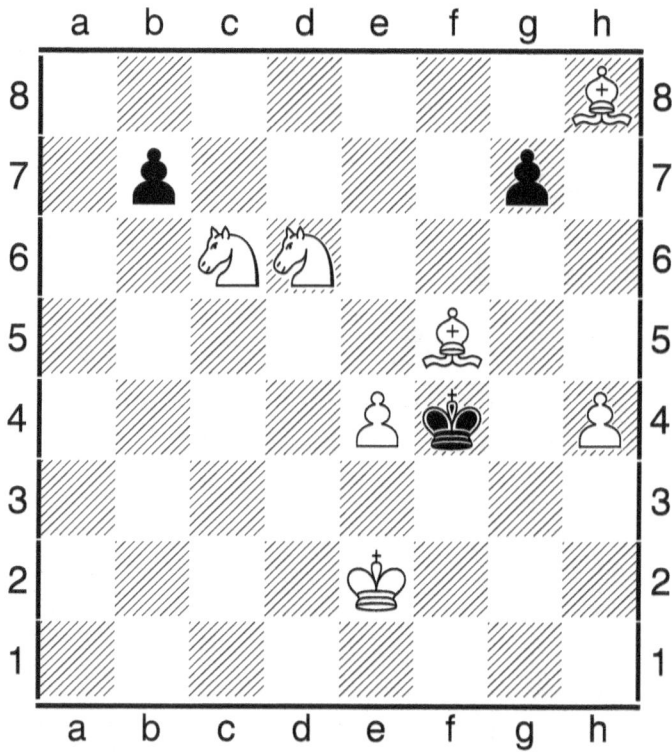

KBBNNPP vs kpp
White is ahead by 12 pawn units (four minor piece's worth) but
can you find the best way to proceed here?

Computer-Generated Chess Problem 01462

White to Play and Mate in 4
Chesthetica v10.46 (Selangor, Malaysia)
Generated on 10 Apr 2017 at 5:42:18 PM
Solvability Estimate = Difficult

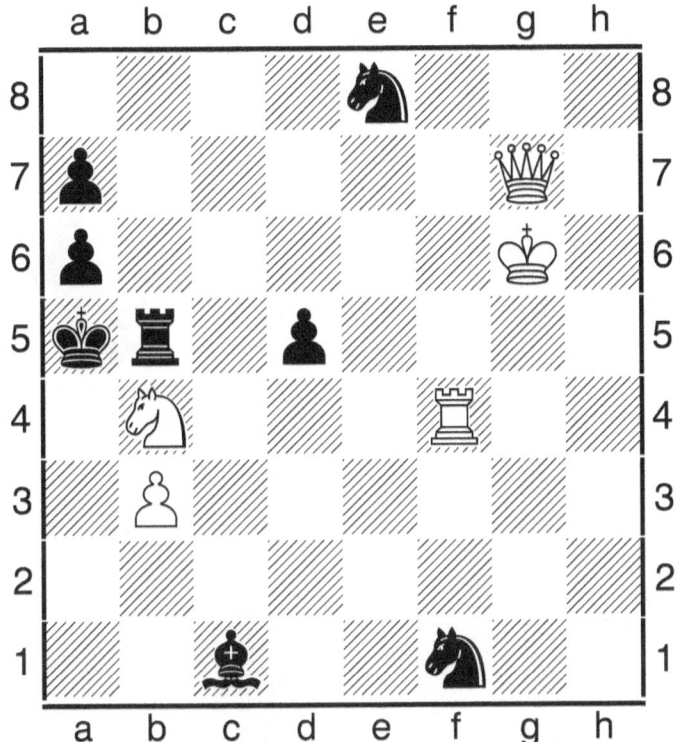

KQRNP vs krbnnppp
White is ahead by one pawn unit but can you find the best way to proceed here?

Computer-Generated Chess Problem 01468

White to Play and Mate in 4
Chesthetica v10.48 (Selangor, Malaysia)
Generated on 17 Apr 2017 at 6:54:33 AM
Solvability Estimate = Difficult

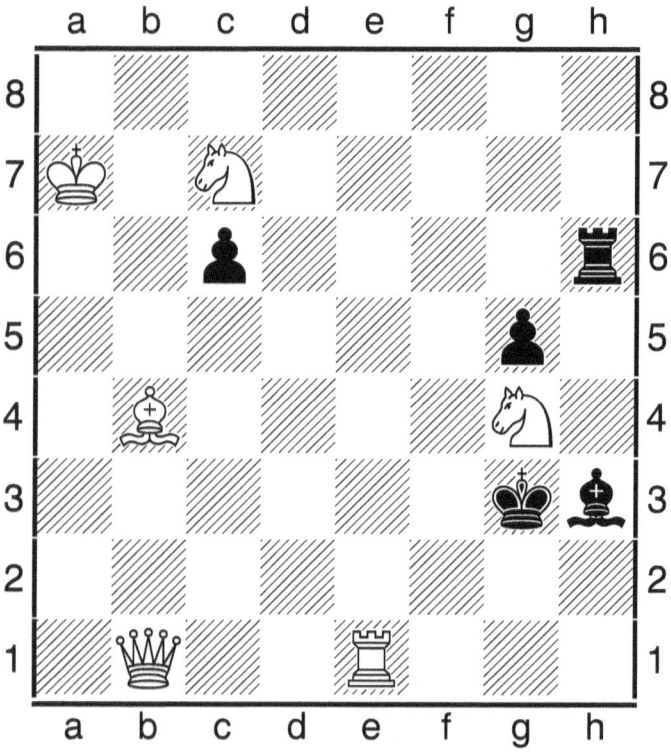

KQRBNN vs krbpp
White is ahead by 13 pawn units but can you find the best way to proceed here?

Computer-Generated Chess Problem 01471

White to Play and Mate in 4
Chesthetica v10.48 (Selangor, Malaysia)
Generated on 19 Apr 2017 at 11:41:20 PM
Solvability Estimate = Easy

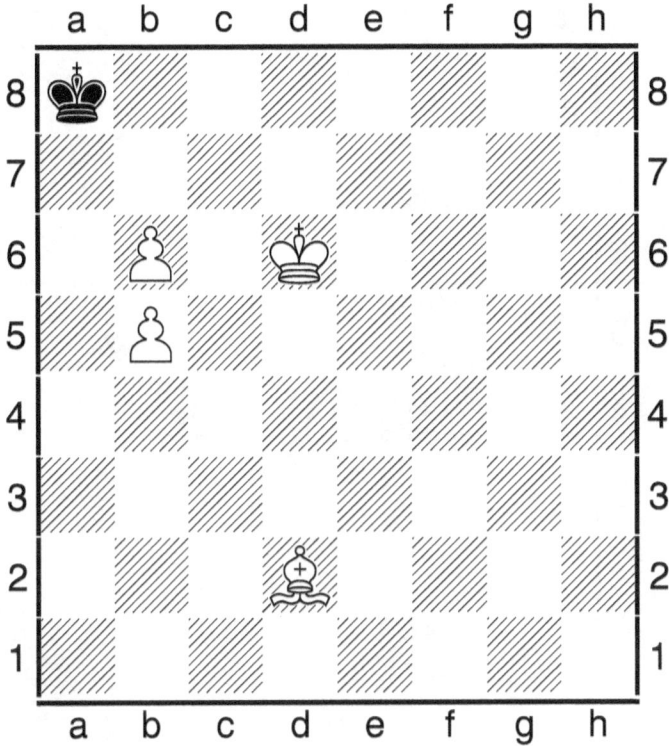

KBPP vs k
White is ahead by five pawn units (a rook's worth) but can you
find the best way to proceed here?

Computer-Generated Chess Problem 01501

White to Play and Mate in 4
Chesthetica v10.48 (Selangor, Malaysia)
Generated on 13 May 2017 at 12:13:59 AM
Solvability Estimate = Difficult

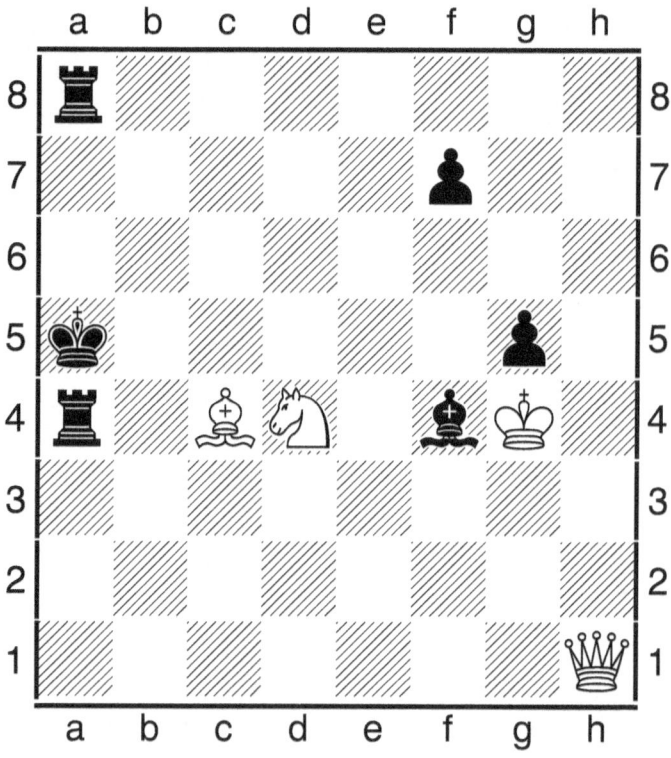

KQBN vs krrbpp
White and Black have the same amount of material.

Computer-Generated Chess Problem 01508

White to Play and Mate in 5
Chesthetica v10.48 (Selangor, Malaysia)
Generated on 16 May 2017 at 8:29:06 PM
Solvability Estimate = Difficult

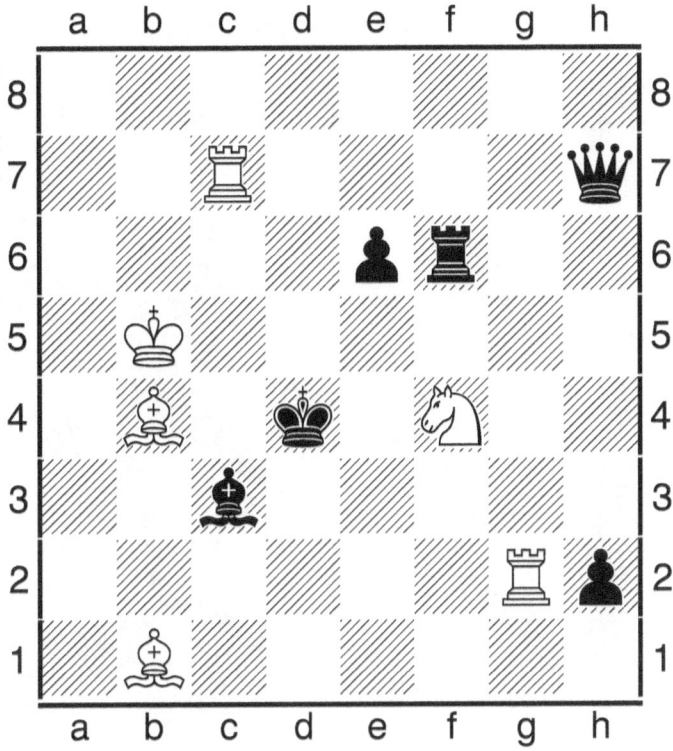

KRRBBN vs kqrbpp
White and Black have the same amount of material. Black is also
close to a pawn promotion.

Computer-Generated Chess Problem 01514

White to Play and Mate in 4
Chesthetica v10.48 (Selangor, Malaysia)
Generated on 22 May 2017 at 5:46:15 AM
Solvability Estimate = Moderate

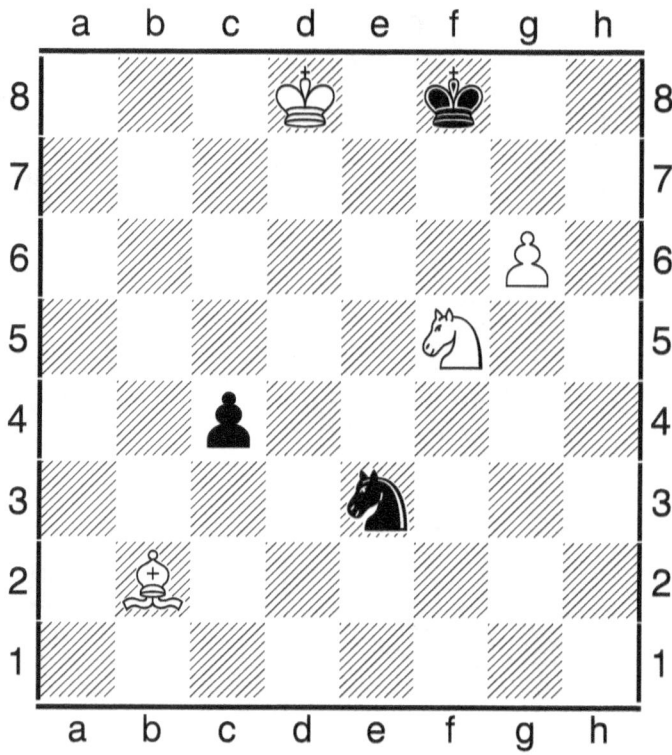

KBNP vs knp
White is ahead by three pawn units (one minor piece's worth) but
can you find the best way to proceed here?

Computer-Generated Chess Problem 01524

White to Play and Mate in 4
Chesthetica v10.48 (Selangor, Malaysia)
Generated on 28 May 2017 at 2:57:45 AM
Solvability Estimate = Moderate

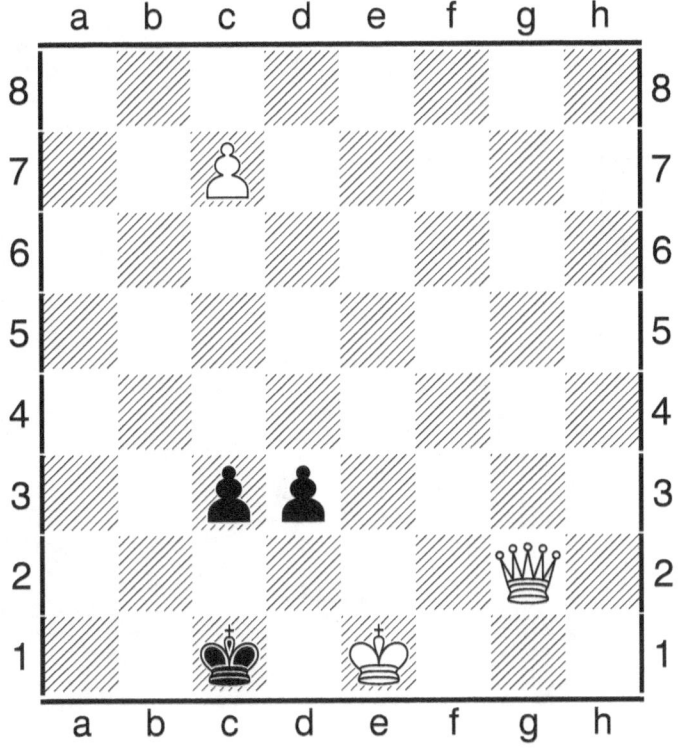

KQP vs kpp
White is ahead by eight pawn units but can you find the best way
to proceed here? White is also close to a pawn promotion.

Computer-Generated Chess Problem 01526

White to Play and Mate in 4
Chesthetica v10.48 (Selangor, Malaysia)
Generated on 30 May 2017 at 11:36:27 AM
Solvability Estimate = Difficult

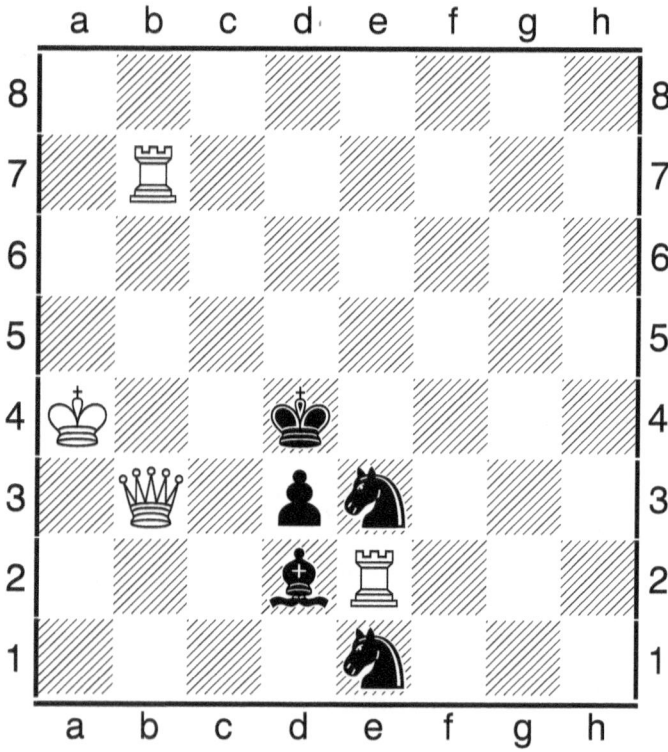

KQRR vs kbnnp
White is ahead by nine pawn units (a queen's worth) but can you find the best way to proceed here?

Chapter 5

Selected Compositions Generated
Between June and August 2017

There is a particularly interesting composition in this chapter which I wrote a whole paper on. Two articles including an online contest (with a prize) where humans were challenged to compose something similar followed it. The one I am referring to is CGCP 01606. Since I abhor redundancy and do my best to avoid it, you may read all about this composition in the references at the end of the book. Suffice to say, however, it was a unique composition that *Chesthetica* was able to compose because not only can *Chesthetica* compose original chess problems but she can also compose based on particular piece sets specified.

This is not something one should take for granted, under any circumstances. Imagine giving someone (e.g. a child, an amateur player, a club player, a master or even a grandmaster) two kings, four white knights and a black queen, then asking the person to compose a forced mate in 5 moves… and to do so *without* the aid of a computer, to make the 'human vs. machine' challenge fair. It is not an easy task for humans. Not even *with* the aid of a computer as the results of the aforementioned contest will also illustrate to you. Then consider that *Chesthetica* can, in principle, compose given *any* combination of pieces and do so 24 hours a day.

Despite all her remarkable capabilities, if I do say so myself, you may instead find gripes by some people (not most people, to be fair) about how her compositions are not 'on the same level' as master compositions. Perhaps their intentions here are noble; that is to say, they hope to see *Chesthetica* 'improve'. The truth, as I have mentioned elsewhere before but in this case it is worth mentioning again, is that I have less interest in traditional compositions such as those. I do find a handful to be particularly fascinating, however, but in general, I tend to enjoy what *Chesthetica* creates more. Perhaps this is partly because I am not a master composer or player myself. Then again, neither are most people in the global chess community.

In the same way that I (or anyone) may appreciate or like a painting by a relative amateur more than most of van Gogh's works, I happen to like what *Chesthetica* creates more than I do most problems by master composers. It is not that I do not think *Chesthetica* has the potential of composing problems like those, it is just that the time and effort needed to take it in that direction does not seem like a good investment to me, in no small part because I do not happen to have the resources of say, IBM or Google to pay for a team of skilled programmers, consultants and the use of very powerful computers, all under my direction and leadership. How do you suppose these corporations could afford to build world-class chess-*playing* programs and even make history?

This may seem like a rant to some, but it is actually an attempt to put into context the mistaken beliefs many people might have about what it takes to actually accomplish certain things in science today. It is far from a straightforward process and most scientific endeavors tend to fail anyway; never mind that most proposals for funding end up rejected to begin with. Regardless, this fifth chapter contains 13 compositions of the forced mate in 3, 4 and 5 varieties. There are no 'easy' ones here, incidentally. They also consist of White having less, equal and more material than Black. If you are looking for a challenge, you are likely in the right place.

Computer-Generated Chess Problem 01532

White to Play and Mate in 4
Chesthetica v10.48 (Selangor, Malaysia)
Generated on 3 Jun 2017 at 2:35:11 AM
Solvability Estimate = Difficult

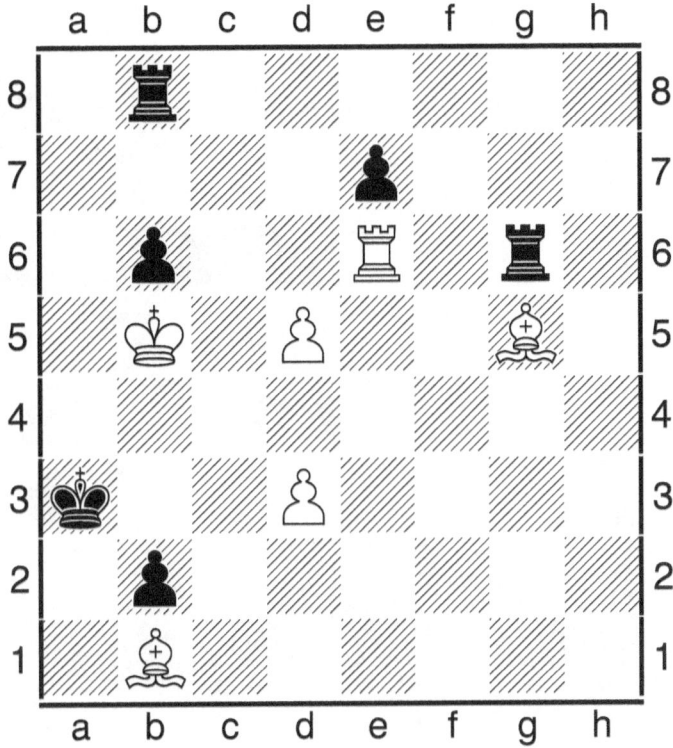

KRBBPP vs krrppp
White and Black have the same amount of material. Black is also close to a pawn promotion.

Computer-Generated Chess Problem 01533

White to Play and Mate in 4
Chesthetica v10.48 (Selangor, Malaysia)
Generated on 3 Jun 2017 at 2:38:56 AM
Solvability Estimate = Difficult

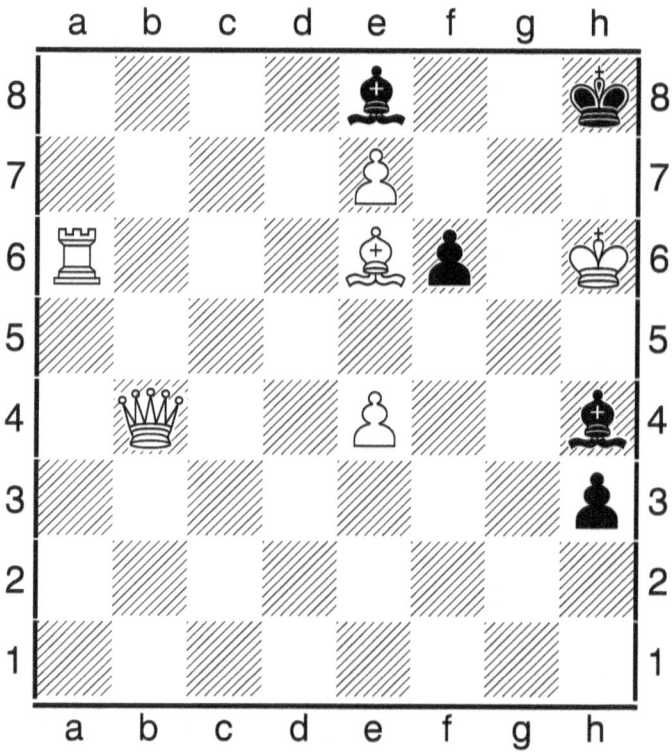

KQRBPP vs kbbpp
White is ahead by 11 pawn units but can you find the best way to
proceed here? White is also close to a pawn promotion.

Computer-Generated Chess Problem 01541

White to Play and Mate in 4
Chesthetica v10.48 (Selangor, Malaysia)
Generated on 9 Jun 2017 at 8:27:02 PM
Solvability Estimate = Moderate

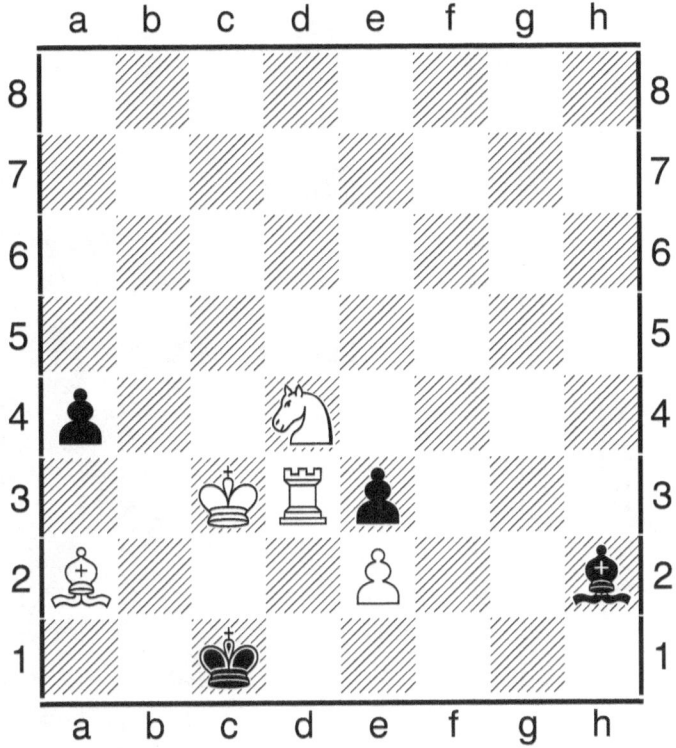

KRBNP vs kbpp
White is ahead by seven pawn units but can you find the best way
to proceed here?

Computer-Generated Chess Problem 01543

White to Play and Mate in 5
Chesthetica v10.48 (Selangor, Malaysia)
Generated on 12 Jun 2017 at 9:57:04 AM
Solvability Estimate = Difficult

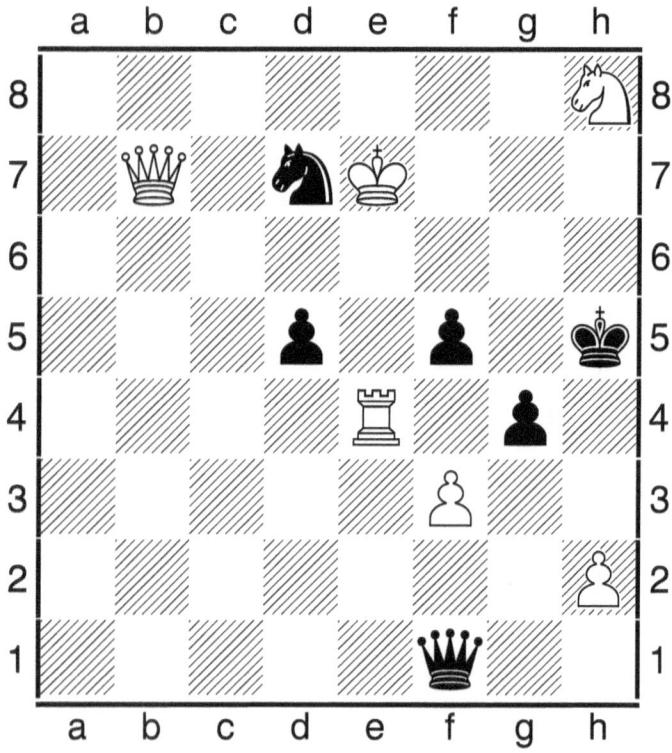

KQRNPP vs kqnppp
White is ahead by four pawn units but can you find the best way
to proceed here?

Computer-Generated Chess Problem 01548

White to Play and Mate in 5
Chesthetica v10.48 (Selangor, Malaysia)
Generated on 16 Jun 2017 at 3:00:45 AM
Solvability Estimate = Difficult

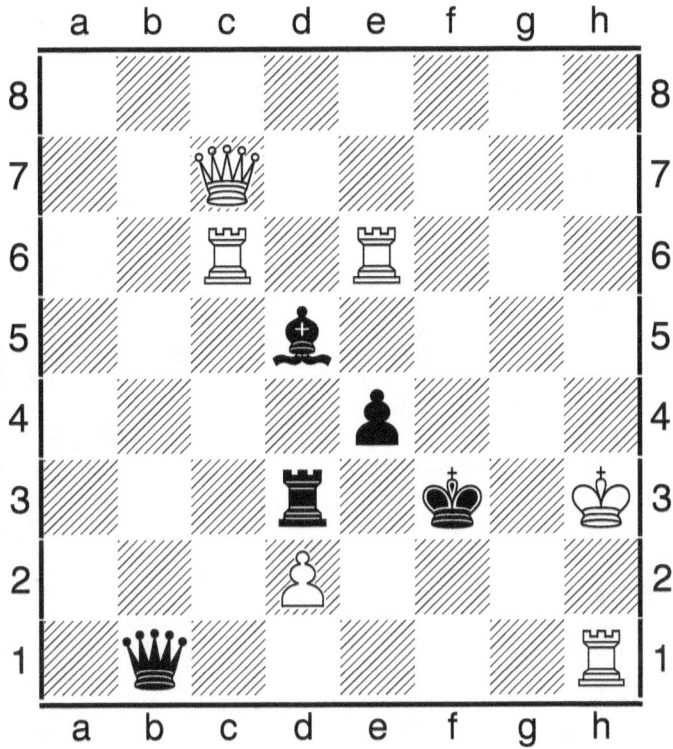

KQRRRP vs kqrbp
White is ahead by seven pawn units but can you find the best way
to proceed here?

Computer-Generated Chess Problem 01552

White to Play and Mate in 4
Chesthetica v10.48 (Selangor, Malaysia)
Generated on 24 Jun 2017 at 4:18:52 AM
Solvability Estimate = Moderate

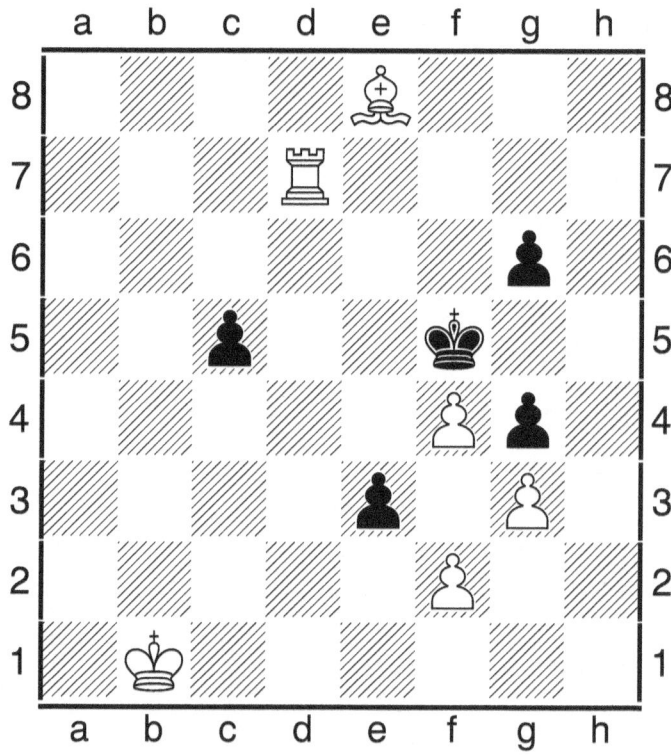

KRBPPP vs kpppp
White is ahead by seven pawn units but can you find the best way
to proceed here?

Computer-Generated Chess Problem 01576

White to Play and Mate in 4
Chesthetica v10.48 (Selangor, Malaysia)
Generated on 17 Jul 2017 at 9:48:35 AM
Solvability Estimate = Difficult

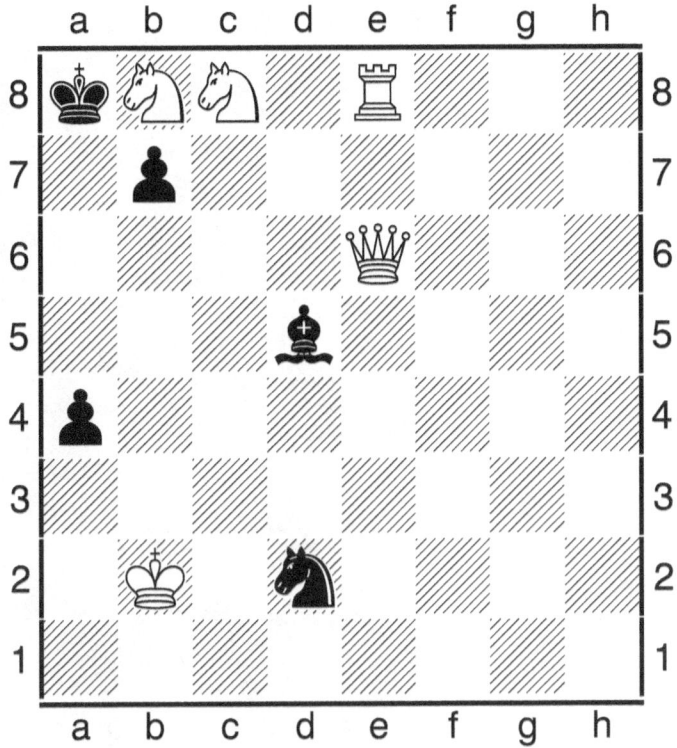

KQRNN vs kbnpp
White is ahead by 12 pawn units (four minor piece's worth) but
can you find the best way to proceed here?

Computer-Generated Chess Problem 01592

White to Play and Mate in 3
Chesthetica v10.51 (Selangor, Malaysia)
Generated on 9 Aug 2017 at 12:09:57 PM
Solvability Estimate = Moderate

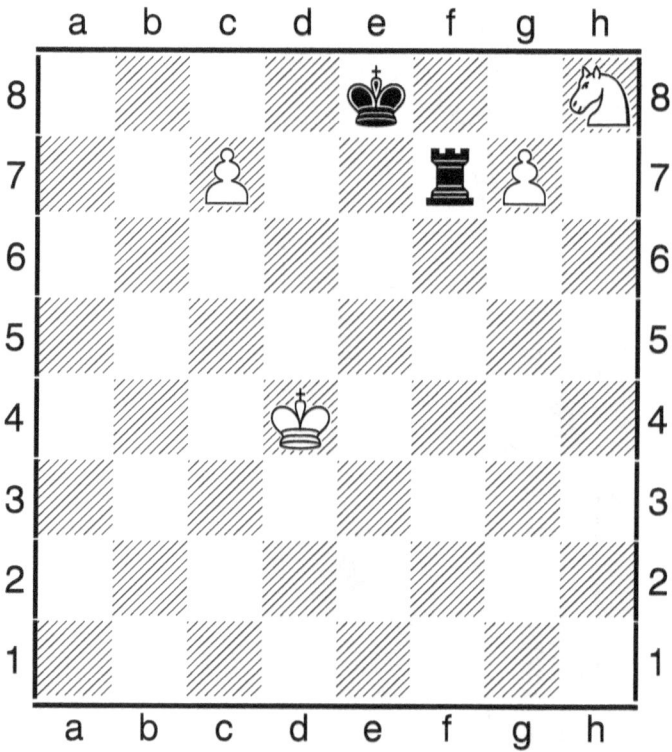

KNPP vs kr
White and Black have the same amount of material. White is also close to a pawn promotion.

Computer-Generated Chess Problem 01598

White to Play and Mate in 3
Chesthetica v10.53 (Selangor, Malaysia)
Generated on 15 Aug 2017 at 11:07:31 AM
Solvability Estimate = Difficult

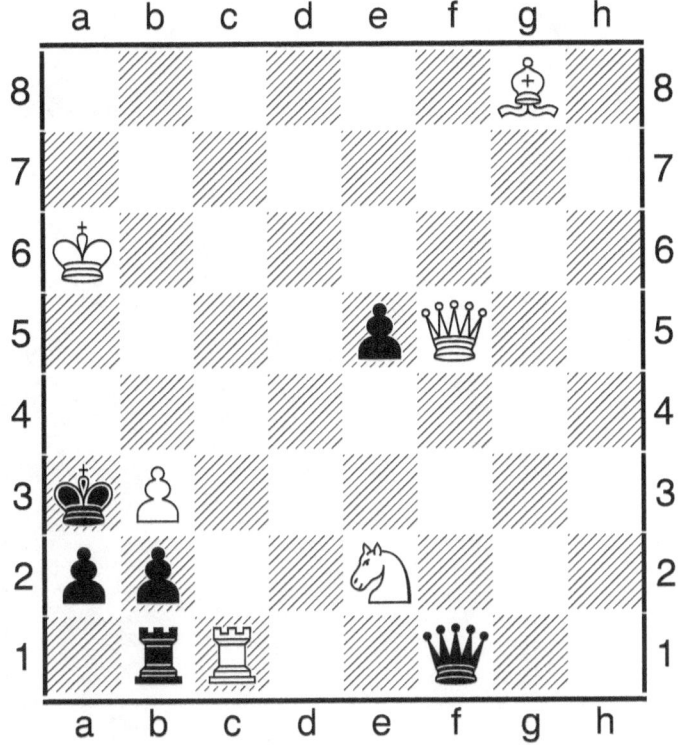

KQRBNP vs kqrppp
White is ahead by four pawn units but can you find the best way
to proceed here? Black is also close to a pawn promotion.

Computer-Generated Chess Problem 01601

White to Play and Mate in 3
Chesthetica v10.53 (Selangor, Malaysia)
Generated on 17 Aug 2017 at 10:49:56 AM
Solvability Estimate = Difficult

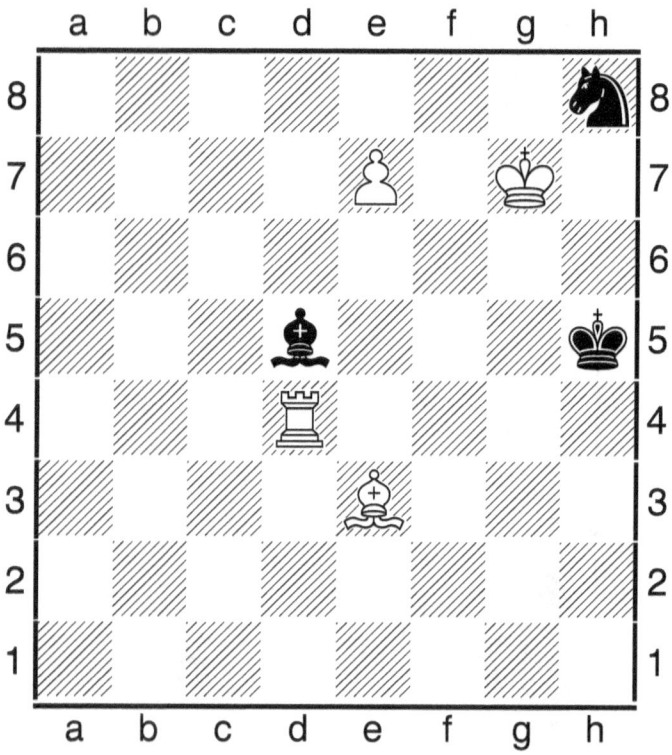

KRBP vs kbn
White is ahead by three pawn units (one minor piece's worth) but
can you find the best way to proceed here? White is also close to
a pawn promotion.

Computer-Generated Chess Problem 01603

White to Play and Mate in 3
Chesthetica v10.53 (Selangor, Malaysia)
Generated on 21 Aug 2017 at 9:11:07 AM
Solvability Estimate = Difficult

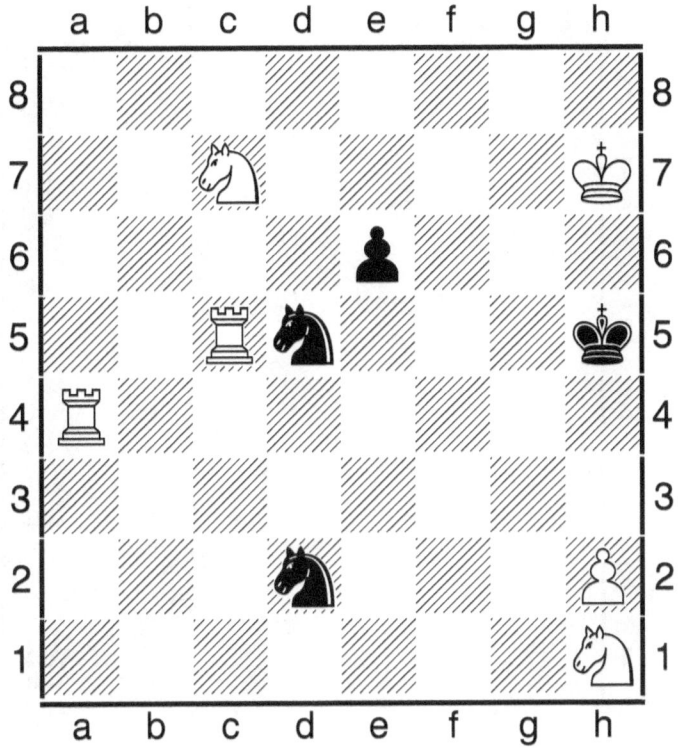

KRRNNP vs knnp
White is ahead by 10 pawn units (two rook's worth) but can you
find the best way to proceed here?

Computer-Generated Chess Problem 01606

White to Play and Mate in 5
Chesthetica v10.53 (Selangor, Malaysia)
Generated on 23 Aug 2017 at 4:51:51 AM
Solvability Estimate = Moderate

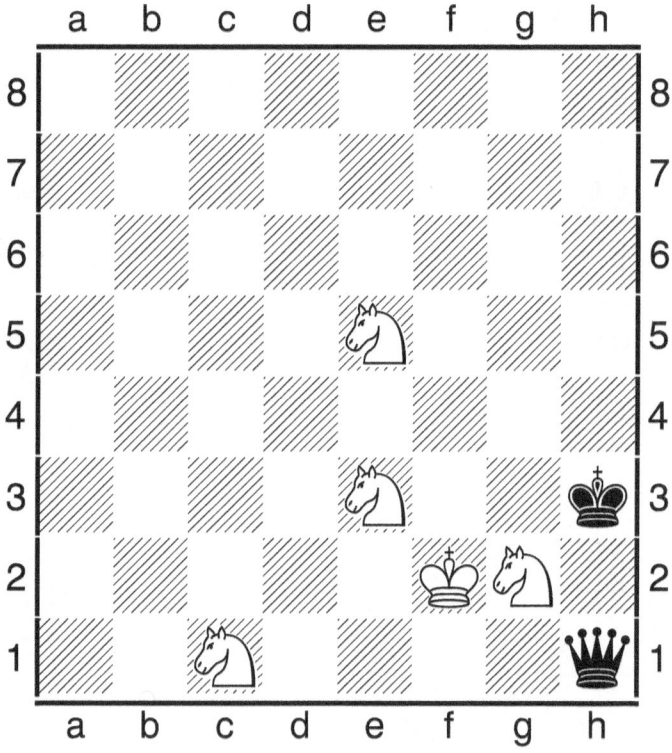

KNNNN vs kq
White is ahead by three pawn units (one minor piece's worth) but can you find the best way to proceed here? There is quite a story behind this one.

Computer-Generated Chess Problem 01611

White to Play and Mate in 3
Chesthetica v10.53 (Selangor, Malaysia)
Generated on 28 Aug 2017 at 5:58:56 PM
Solvability Estimate = Difficult

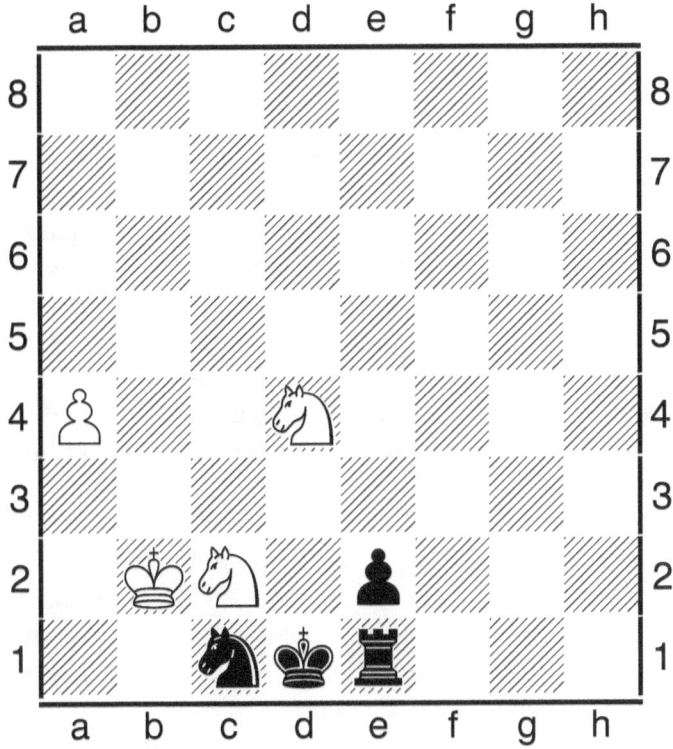

KNNP vs krnp
White is actually down by two pawn units. Black is also close to a pawn promotion.

Chapter 6

Selected Compositions Generated Between September and November 2017

If you read about CGCP 01606 in the previous chapter, you should know that CGCP 01635 is related to that story. To put it briefly, I wanted to demonstrate that the four knights versus queen (7 pieces, including the kings) was not taken from an endgame tablebase. Therefore I instead replaced the black queen with two black rooks and made it 8 pieces, in total. When this piece combination was fed into *Chesthetica* to compose with, it also succeeded as shown in CGCP 01635. Granted, the composition itself is nothing particularly spectacular but it is still a valid one and again, is not something anyone would be able to compose at a whim.

Given these remarkable capabilities, one might ask why has not a large corporation like IBM or Google pursued automatic chess composition or even approached me to take *Chesthetica* (or the DSNS approach) even further given all their available resources? The answer is likely quite simple. They probably do not see what it would prove. A computer that composes chess problems? So what? Who really cares? On the other hand, they might be interested in the DSNS computational creativity approach behind it. Alas, until I or someone else has also demonstrated *that* to be useful beyond the domain of chess problem composition (say, in protein folding), they have no reason to believe it will work either.

The right mix of opportunities, resources and timing are required for any scientific enterprise to truly succeed. The best I can do, perhaps, given my personal circumstances, is to keep doing what I am doing until sufficient interest brews to take the DSNS approach into other domains where it can be tested. On a personal level, I am far from destitute (thankfully), and therefore the pursuit of more wealth through this technology has not really been a major motivation of mine. I would be fairly satisfied, for instance, seeing it do some real good, beyond chess problem composition, and contribute to the field of AI, in general. Even if nothing more happens, I am still enthralled by what Chesthetica keeps creating and it is a source of constant joy for me. So is continuing to work on its code, believe it or not.

Scientific breakthroughs, if we may borrow that term loosely here, often take decades or even centuries to permeate society, if it happens at all. I should hope that by saying this, I am also clarifying to interested parties why things are the way they are. So, what can I now say about chapter 6 to get back on track with this volume? It is the longest chapter and most of the compositions are of the mate in 3 variety, even though all the other types are here too. None of these are 'easy' either, even though the one study-like construct might be. Not because I personally think so but because there is no solvability estimate for it. With this chapter, however, you are literally closest to the solutions.

Computer-Generated Chess Problem 01624

White to Play and Mate in 3
Chesthetica v10.53 (Selangor, Malaysia)
Generated on 7 Sep 2017 at 8:34:39 PM
Solvability Estimate = Difficult

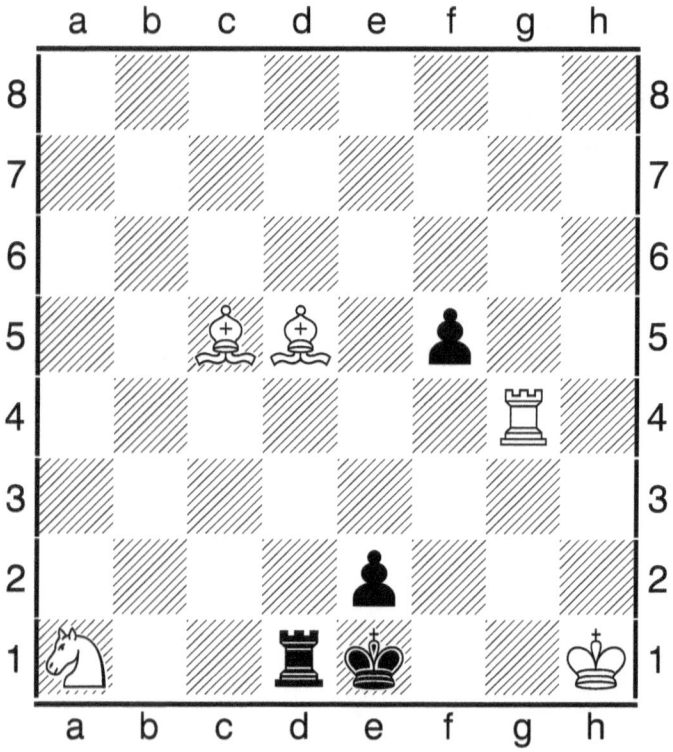

KRBBN vs krpp
White is ahead by seven pawn units but can you find the best way
to proceed here? Black is also close to a pawn promotion.

Computer-Generated Chess Problem 01634

White to Play and Mate in 4
Chesthetica v10.53 (Selangor, Malaysia)
Generated on 16 Sep 2017 at 1:50:47 PM
Solvability Estimate = Difficult

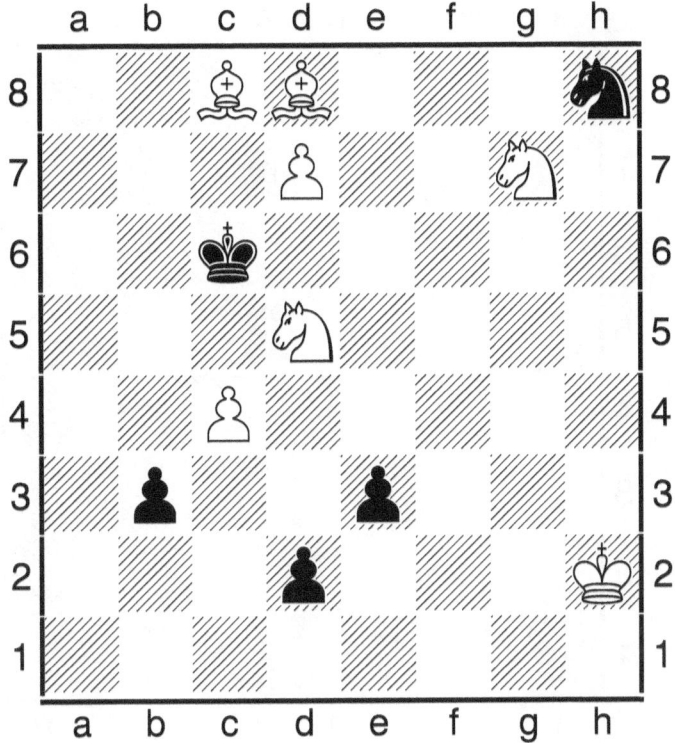

KBBNNPP vs knppp
White is ahead by eight pawn units but can you find the best way
to proceed here? White is also close to a pawn promotion but so
is Black.

Computer-Generated Chess Problem 01635

White to Play and Mate in 5
Chesthetica v10.56 (Selangor, Malaysia)
Generated on 27 Sep 2017 at 5:44:32 AM
Solvability Estimate = Moderate

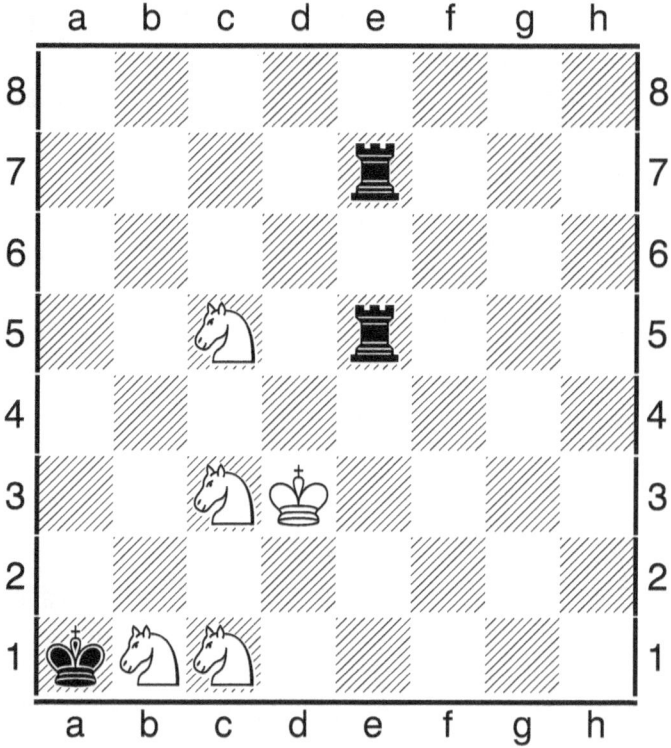

KNNNN vs krr
White is ahead by two pawn units but can you find the best way
to proceed here? This problem is related to CGCP 01606.

Computer-Generated Chess Problem 01638

White to Play and Mate in 3
Chesthetica v10.56 (Selangor, Malaysia)
Generated on 2 Oct 2017 at 3:56:34 AM
Solvability Estimate = Moderate

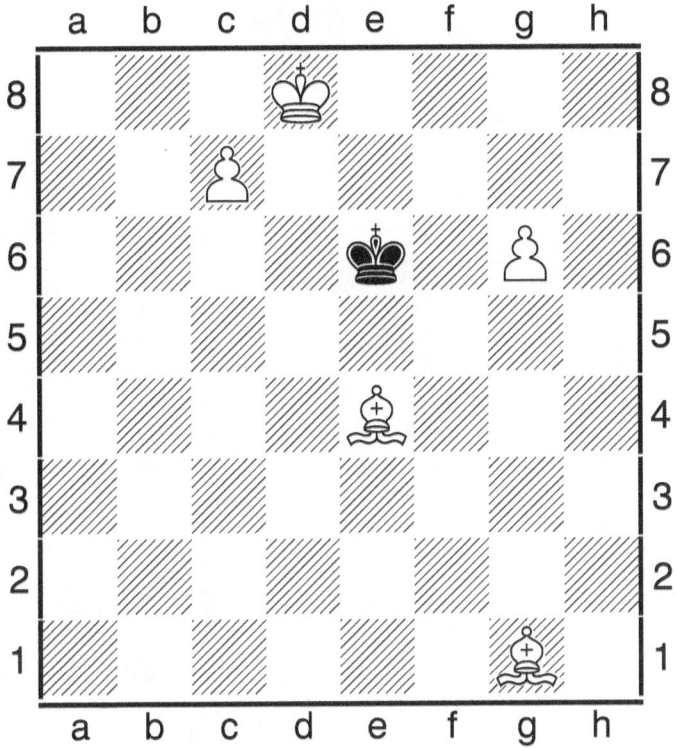

KBBPP vs k
White is ahead by eight pawn units but can you find the best way
to proceed here? White is also close to a pawn promotion.

Computer-Generated Chess Problem 01646

White to Play and Mate in 3
Chesthetica v10.56 (Selangor, Malaysia)
Generated on 4 Oct 2017 at 11:30:36 PM
Solvability Estimate = Moderate

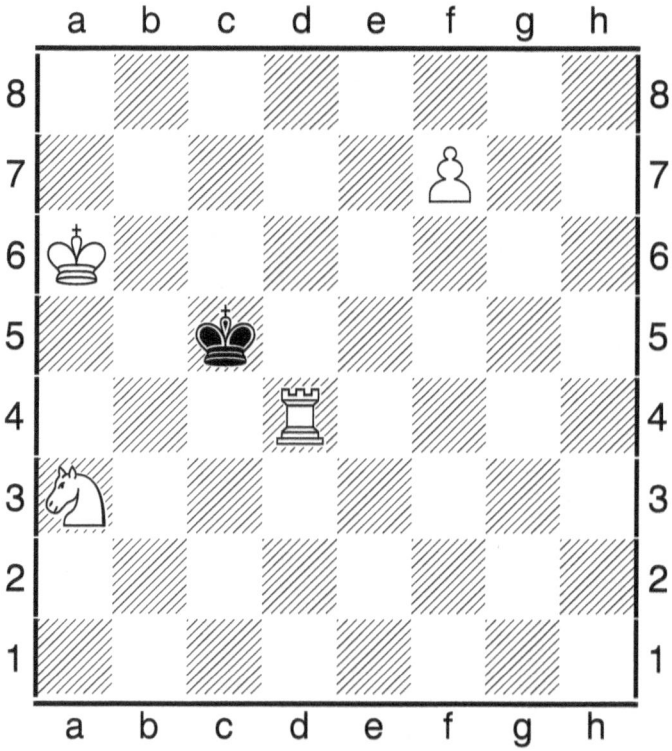

KRNP vs k

White is ahead by nine pawn units (a queen's worth) but can you find the best way to proceed here? White is also close to a pawn promotion.

Computer-Generated Chess Problem 01653

White to Play and Mate in 4
Chesthetica v10.56 (Selangor, Malaysia)
Generated on 6 Oct 2017 at 10:01:10 PM
Solvability Estimate = Moderate

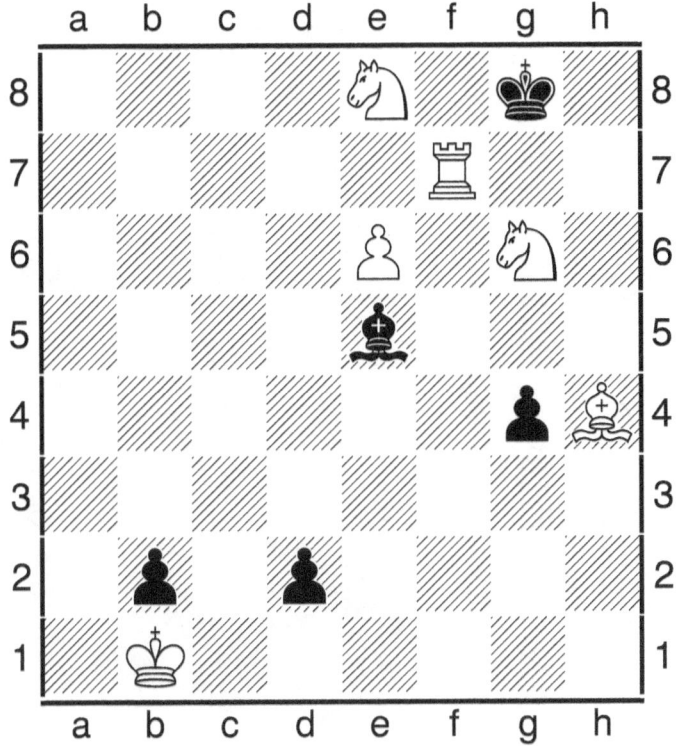

KRBNNP vs kbppp
White is ahead by nine pawn units (a queen's worth) but can you find the best way to proceed here? Black is also close to a pawn promotion.

Computer-Generated Chess Problem 01657

White to Play and Mate in 3
Chesthetica v10.56 (Selangor, Malaysia)
Generated on 8 Oct 2017 at 1:25:35 PM
Solvability Estimate = Difficult

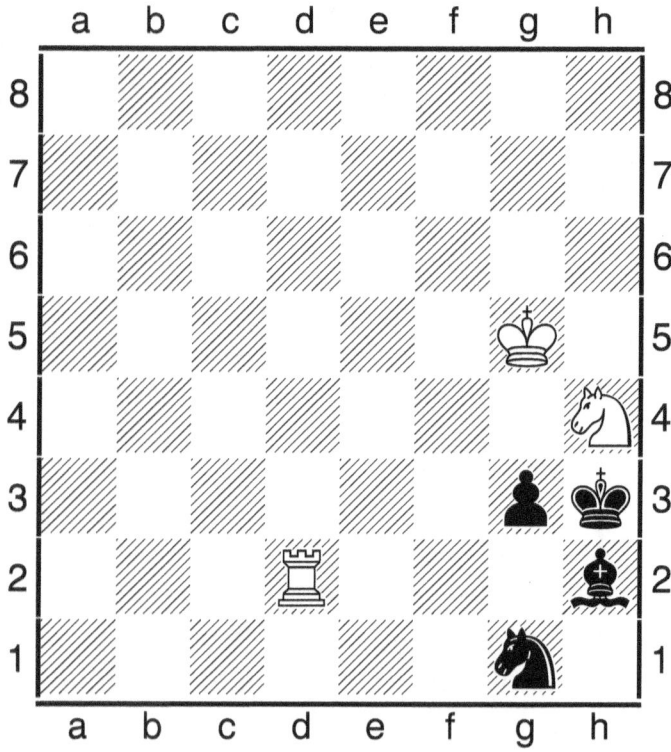

KRN vs kbnp
White is ahead by one pawn unit but can you find the best way to proceed here?

Computer-Generated Chess Problem 01659

White to Play and Mate in 3
Chesthetica v10.56 (Selangor, Malaysia)
Generated on 9 Oct 2017 at 1:52:34 AM
Solvability Estimate = Difficult

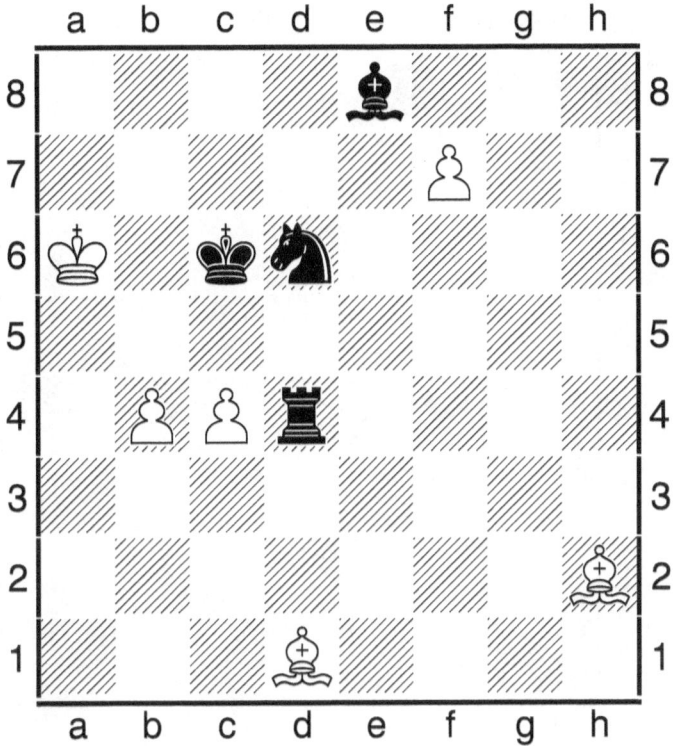

KBBPPP vs krbn
White is actually down by two pawn units. White is also close to a pawn promotion.

Computer-Generated Chess Problem 01672

White to Play and Mate in 3
Chesthetica v10.56 (Selangor, Malaysia)
Generated on 13 Oct 2017 at 11:38:56 PM
Solvability Estimate = Moderate

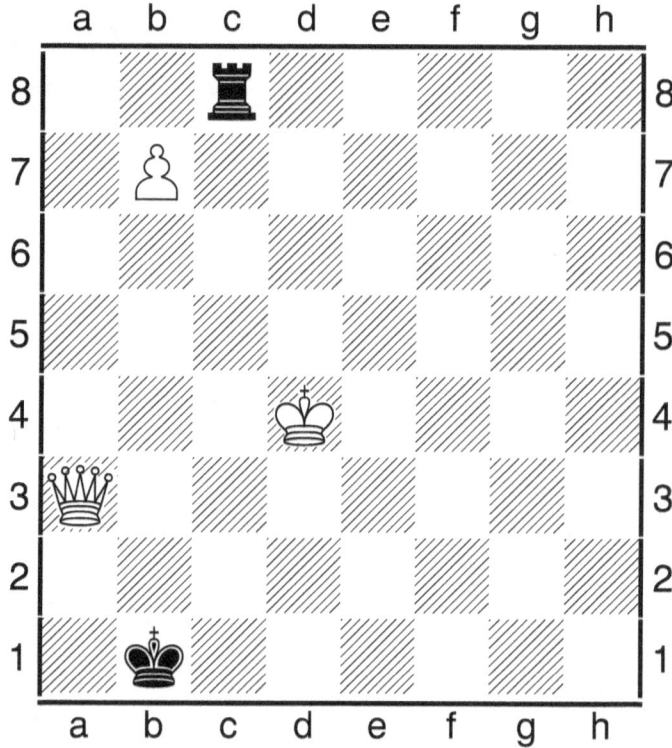

KQP vs kr
White is ahead by five pawn units (a rook's worth) but can you find the best way to proceed here? White is also close to a pawn promotion.

Computer-Generated Chess Problem 01675

White to Play and Mate in 3
Chesthetica v10.56 (Selangor, Malaysia)
Generated on 15 Oct 2017 at 2:53:35 PM
Solvability Estimate = Difficult

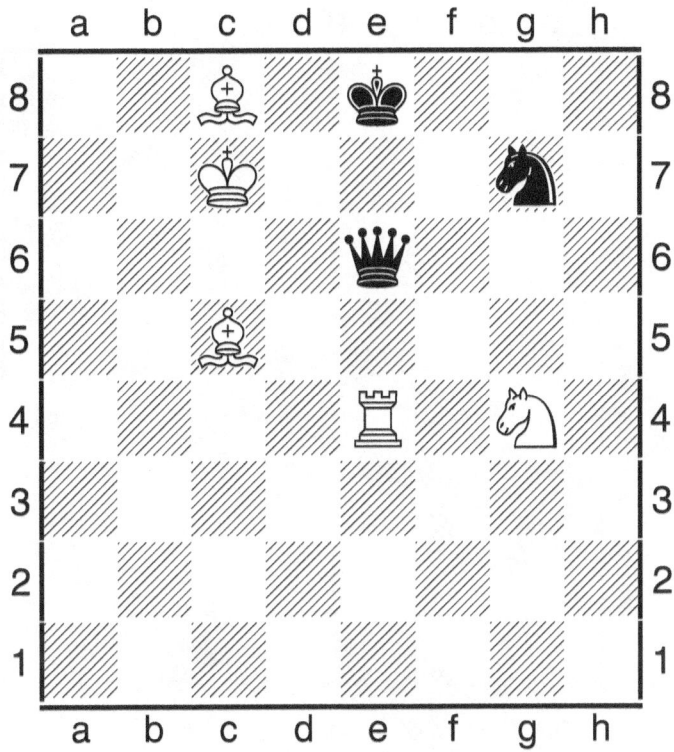

KRBBN vs kqn
White is ahead by two pawn units but can you find the best way
to proceed here?

Computer-Generated Chess Problem 01700

White to Play and Win
Chesthetica v10.56 (Selangor, Malaysia)
Generated on 30 Oct 2017 at 10:59:57 PM

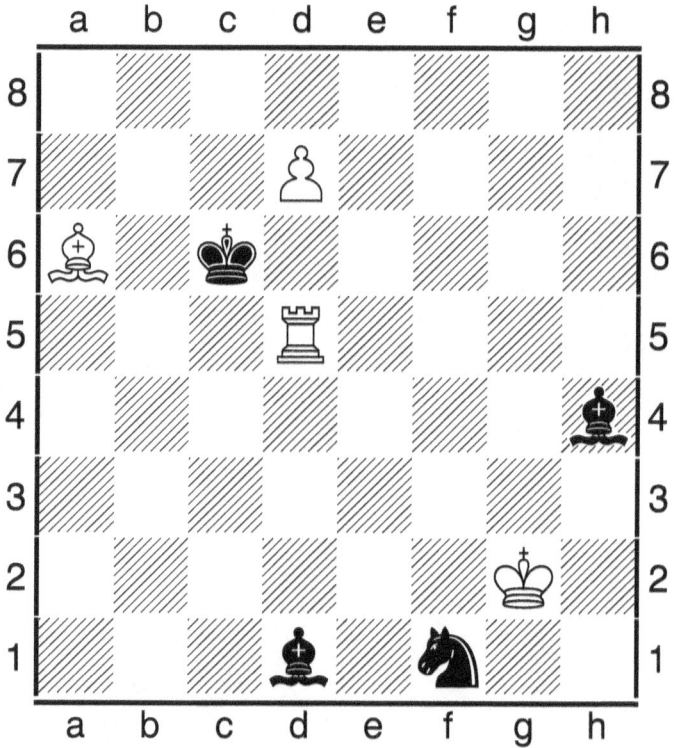

KRBP vs kbbn
White and Black have the same amount of material. White is also
close to a pawn promotion.

Computer-Generated Chess Problem 01703

White to Play and Mate in 3
Chesthetica v10.56 (Selangor, Malaysia)
Generated on 3 Nov 2017 at 7:59:57 PM
Solvability Estimate = Difficult

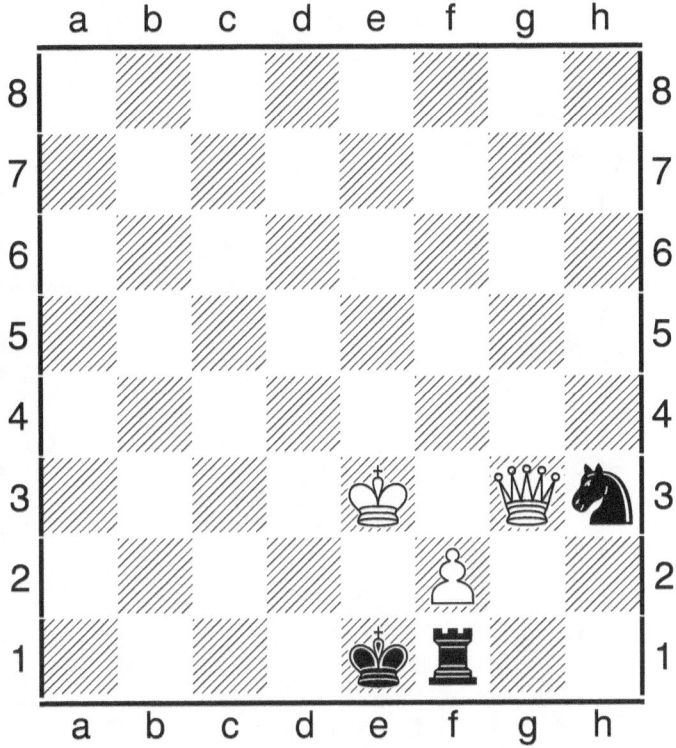

KQP vs krn
White is ahead by two pawn units but can you find the best way
to proceed here?

Computer-Generated Chess Problem 01719

White to Play and Mate in 4
Chesthetica v10.56 (Selangor, Malaysia)
Generated on 14 Nov 2017 at 8:53:34 PM
Solvability Estimate = Difficult

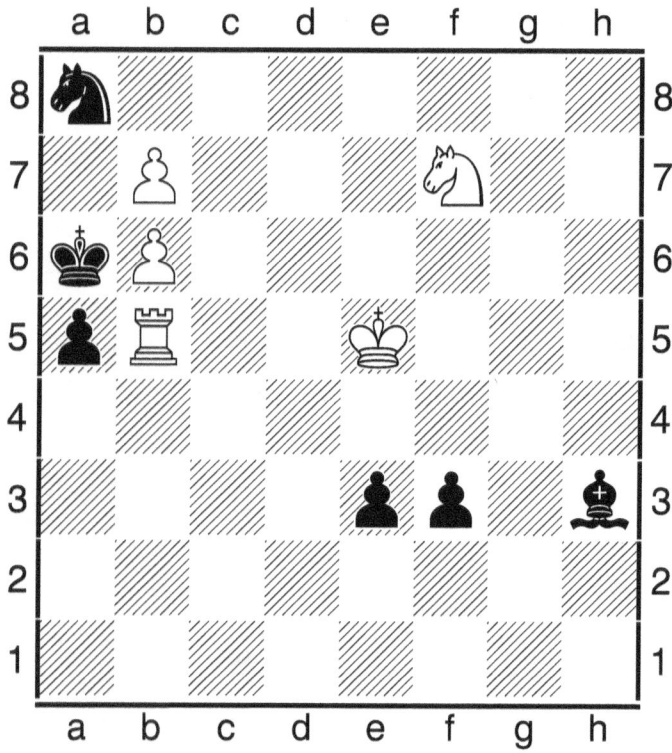

KRNPP vs kbnppp
White is ahead by one pawn unit but can you find the best way to
proceed here? White is also close to a pawn promotion.

Computer-Generated Chess Problem 01726

White to Play and Mate in 5
Chesthetica v10.57 (Selangor, Malaysia)
Generated on 16 Nov 2017 at 7:10:44 PM
Solvability Estimate = Moderate

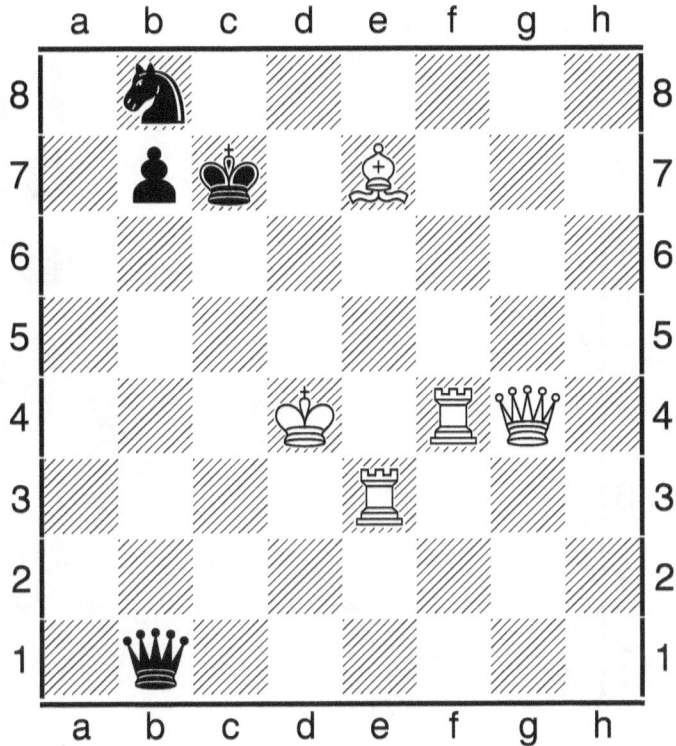

KQRRB vs kqnp
White is ahead by nine pawn units (a queen's worth) but can you find the best way to proceed here?

Computer-Generated Chess Problem 01729

White to Play and Mate in 3
Chesthetica v10.57 (Selangor, Malaysia)
Generated on 18 Nov 2017 at 4:45:15 PM
Solvability Estimate = Difficult

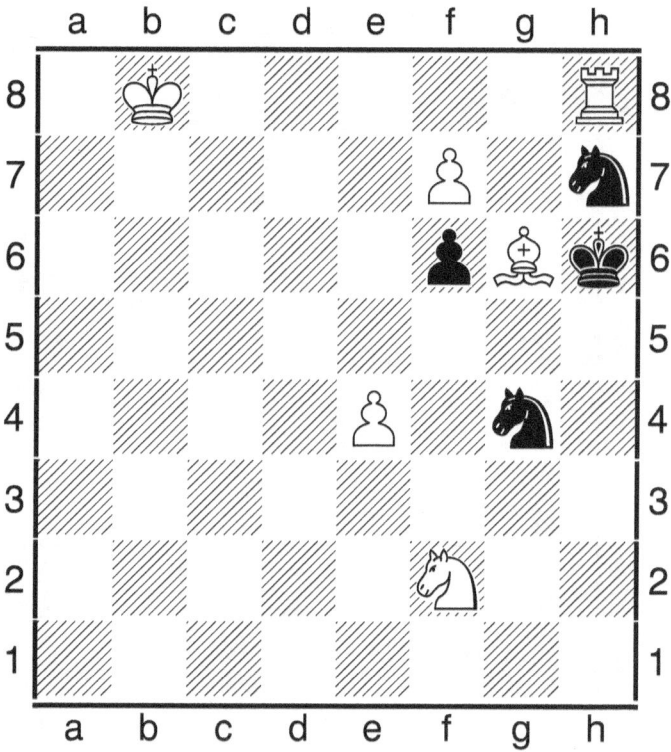

KRBNPP vs knnp
White is ahead by six pawn units (two minor piece's worth) but
can you find the best way to proceed here? White is also close to
a pawn promotion.

Computer-Generated Chess Problem 01734

White to Play and Mate in 3
Chesthetica v10.57 (Selangor, Malaysia)
Generated on 21 Nov 2017 at 3:14:40 AM
Solvability Estimate = Difficult

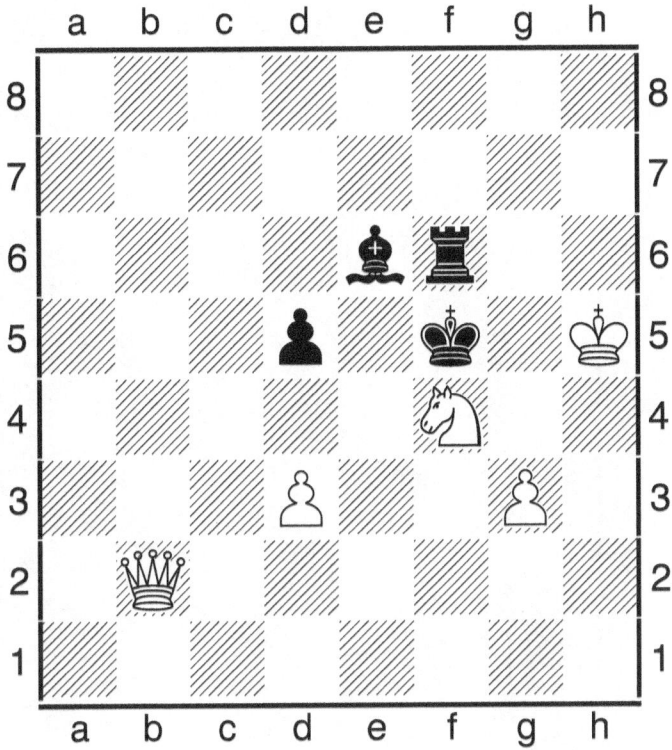

KQNPP vs krbp
White is ahead by five pawn units (a rook's worth) but can you find the best way to proceed here?

Computer-Generated Chess Problem 01737

White to Play and Mate in 3
Chesthetica v10.57 (Selangor, Malaysia)
Generated on 21 Nov 2017 at 3:44:19 PM
Solvability Estimate = Difficult

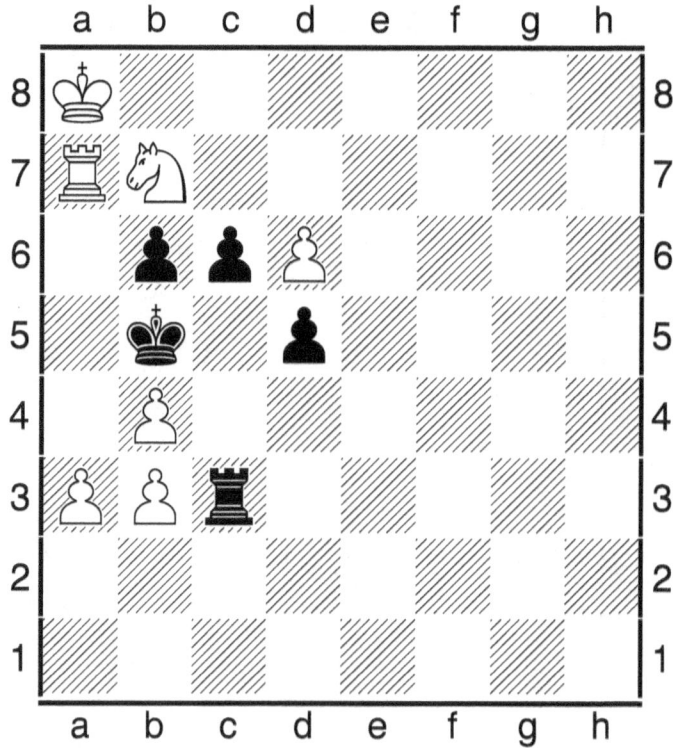

KRNPPPP vs krppp
White is ahead by four pawn units but can you find the best way
to proceed here?

Computer-Generated Chess Problem 01740

White to Play and Mate in 3
Chesthetica v10.57 (Selangor, Malaysia)
Generated on 22 Nov 2017 at 3:41:39 PM
Solvability Estimate = Difficult

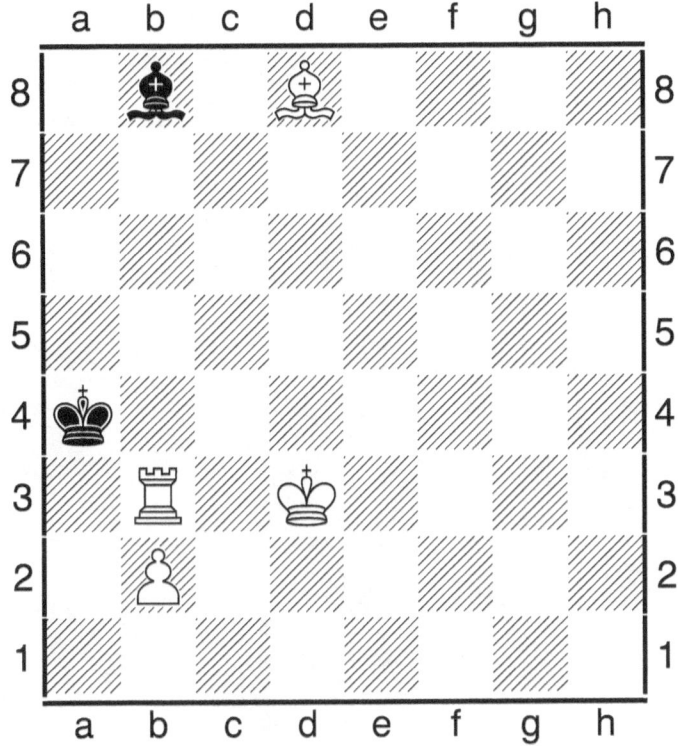

KRBP vs kb
White is ahead by six pawn units (two minor piece's worth) but
can you find the best way to proceed here?

Computer-Generated Chess Problem 01746

White to Play and Mate in 3
Chesthetica v10.57 (Selangor, Malaysia)
Generated on 26 Nov 2017 at 3:20:19 AM
Solvability Estimate = Difficult

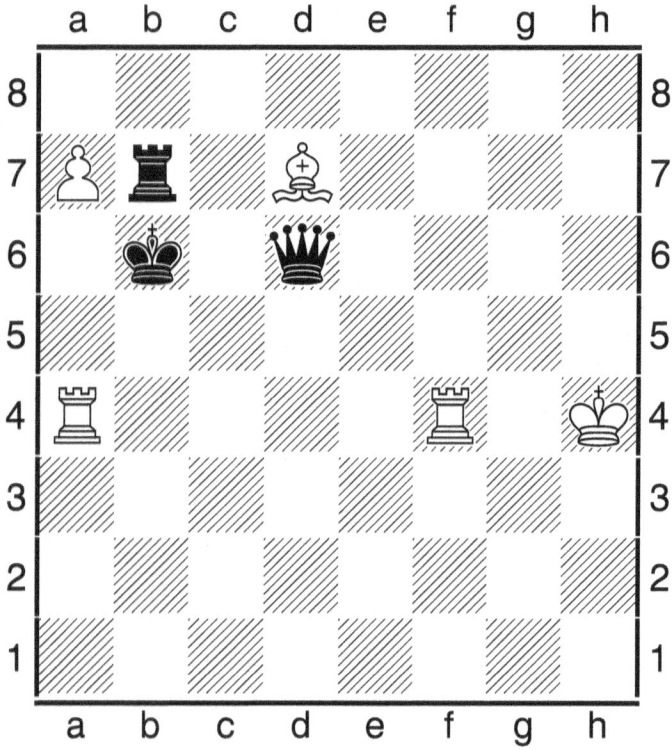

KRRBP vs kqr
White and Black have the same amount of material. White is also close to a pawn promotion.

Computer-Generated Chess Problem 01747

White to Play and Mate in 3
Chesthetica v10.57 (Selangor, Malaysia)
Generated on 27 Nov 2017 at 12:18:48 AM
Solvability Estimate = Difficult

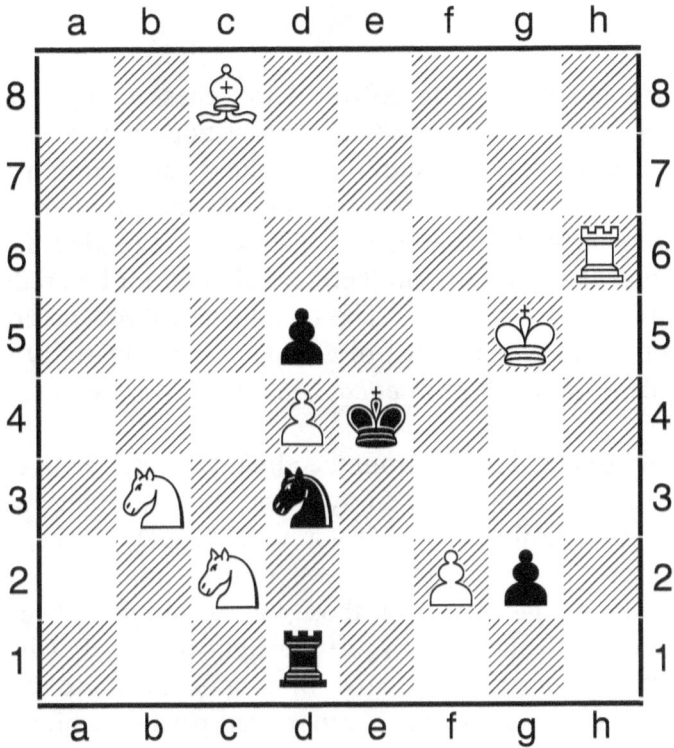

KRBNNPP vs krnpp
White is ahead by six pawn units (two minor piece's worth) but
can you find the best way to proceed here? Black is also close to a
pawn promotion.

Chapter 7

Solutions and Analyses

If you actually tried to solve all the chess compositions before arriving here, I salute and thank you. I hope you enjoyed them. If you could not solve most of them (quickly enough or at all), do not be too concerned. It may simply mean the problems were more challenging than you expected. Please be reminded that I did not compose them myself and therefore should not be credited for my 'creativity' in that regard. The compositions you just experienced are completely the product of computational creativity which even I, the developer of *Chesthetica*, could not have predicted.

I merely selected some (from the already-filtered online collection) that I myself particularly enjoyed and thought others would too; a subset suitable for a book, if you will. In making such a selection (even for the larger online set), I must admit that many such compositions, perhaps even those that would have been appealing to others, will likely never see the light of day. If I have learned one thing from posting now thousands of these compositions online via social media, I can never predict which ones most people will 'like' the most. The overall feedback has been quite positive and I have even learned a thing or two about what people tend to prefer, in general (see the reference section at the end of the book for a link to a related article on this subject).

You may be wondering how come someone or some corporation with access to more resources and expertise has not come out with a better or more capable software than *Chesthetica*. One that maybe has even master composers[1] 'resigning' en masse. After all, it has already been a decade since the first computer-generated chess problem was produced autonomously (i.e. no human intervention in the composition process). One reason may be the lack of interest in the subject (as I alluded to earlier) but another may be that artificial intelligence, perhaps science in general, is not 'progressing exponentially' as we are so often today led to believe. When something new like *Chesthetica* comes out, or even the idea of such a thing is reported somewhere, there will be many who will automatically assume that within a few years the technology (in much better form to boot) will be everywhere, i.e. available, accessible and affordable to all.

An idea, even a prototype (as *Chesthetica* remains to this day), may be one thing but effective commercialization and proliferation of a technology into public life (e.g. strong chess engines today) may take much longer, if it happens at all. Speaking as an academic, research grants are not as generous as they used to be even ten years ago. There are far more restrictions now. Not only in terms of what funding bodies 'prefer' to finance (usually something more in line with national or industry 'needs') but also in terms of what the researcher can do with the funds. Often, what used to be permitted, e.g. attending conferences overseas and buying books, are no longer allowed or far more restrictive.

In some cases, even in computer-related research, the purchase of computers or software is not allowed, if you can believe that. The grants are also a lot smaller than they used to be and a lot harder to obtain. Not only is all this highly demotivating but it also points to a new world in which purely academic research is losing more and more ground to 'prioritized' research topics. This unfortunately ignores what has led to some of the greatest breakthroughs in

---

[1] Incidentally, the renowned grandmaster and composer, Pál Benkö, shortly before his passing, decided to review a few of *Chesthetica's* compositions up to that point (not at my request) and in the same article announced he was dropping out of problem competitions. I hope *Chesthetica* had nothing to do with that decision but I cannot be sure (see the reference section at the end of the book for the article).

science, i.e. 'accidents' or happenstance that stem from unexpected and often unrelated areas of inquiry. The things that take us on tangents we would otherwise never have knowingly pursued.

Perhaps it was inevitable that this would be the eventual state of affairs in science. Even the term 'breakthrough' today is so bastardized many in science actually believe every other conference or journal paper published is a breakthrough. I perhaps should not complain too much about this since I did at least manage to catch a sliver of the 'old school' approach to science in academia and it was sufficient to lead to the development of *Chesthetica*. This might therefore help explain why no one even in the last decade has come up with an alternative, much less a better program. This includes many existing chess software packages that people might think could be easily 'enhanced' to include an automatic composing feature.

It is simply not the kind of topic or research direction that would get the support of a typical academic or funding institution, be it in the public or private sector, if the distinction even exists anymore. Furthermore, most academic journals 'of repute' today would rather not publish research in such an area because they fear it will not get cited as often and affect their precious 'impact factor'. Perhaps this will help the layman understand the constraints faced when it comes to research like this. In AI, especially, chess (*playing*, at least) has remained king since the field's inception and a preferred domain of investigation but less so, as the years and decades go by. Where all this will lead remains to be seen.

Now for the solutions. I have made some minor changes compared to the previous volume. The main line (also chosen by *Chesthetica*) is still in bold font but the variations are now shown below it starting from move 1. This may be seen as somewhat redundant but I do believe it makes it easier to read. The size of the typeface has also been adjusted individually for each problem's solution so that they fit efficiently into a page. In most cases this means two per page but in other cases a whole page or slightly more. A smaller version of the board is also provided (again) so you do not have to flip back and forth to imagine what the solution would look like on the board. This is perhaps ironically more cumbersome in the e-book than the printed version.

CGCP 01071

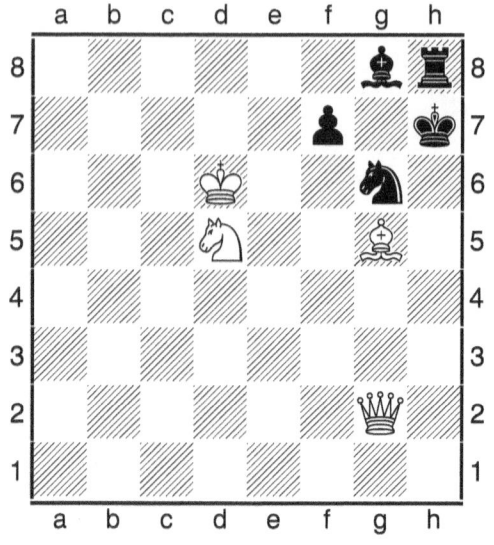

**1. Bf6 Kh6 2. Qg5+
Kh7 3. Qh5#**
1. Bf6 Ne5 2. Qg7#
1. Bf6 Nf8 2. Qg7#
1. Bf6 Nf4 2. Qg7#
1. Bf6 Nh4 2. Qg7#
1. Bf6 Ne7 2. Qg7#

CGCP 01077

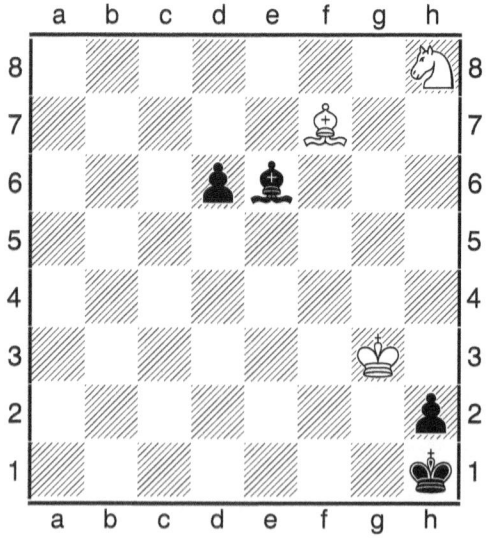

1. Kf2 Bxf7 2. Nxf7 d5 3. Nd6
d4 4. Ne4 d3 5. Ng3#
1. Kf2 Bxf7 2. Nxf7 d5 3. Nd6
d4 4. Nf5 d3 5. Ng3#
1. Kf2 Bxf7 2. Nxf7 d5 3. Ng5
d4 4. Ne4 d3 5. Ng3#
1. Kf2 Bxf7 2. Nxf7 d5 3. Nh6
d4 4. Nf5 d3 5. Ng3#
1. Kf2 Bc4 2. Bxc4 d5 3. Bxd5#
1. Kf2 Bb3 2. Bxb3 d5 3. Bxd5#
1. Kf2 Ba2 2. Bxa2 d5 3. Bxd5#
1. Kf2 Bf5 2. Bd5+ Be4 3. Bxe4#
1. Kf2 Bg4 2. Bd5+ Bf3 3. Bxf3#
1. Kf2 Bh3 2. Bd5+ Bg2 3.
Bxg2#
1. Kf2 d5 2. Bxe6 d4 3. Bd5#
1. Kf2 Bd7 2. Bd5#
1. Kf2 Bc8 2. Bd5#
1. Kf2 Bd5 2. Bxd5#

CGCP 01084

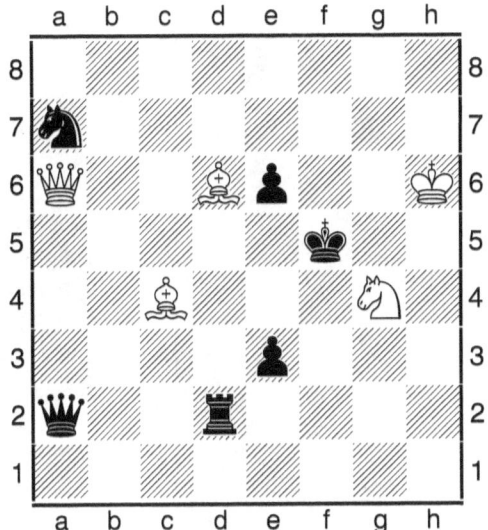

1. Qb7 Rh2+ 2. Nxh2 Qxh2+ 3. Bxh2 Kf6 4. Qg7+ Kf5 5. Bd3#
1. Qb7 Rh2+ 2. Nxh2 Qxh2+ 3. Bxh2 Nc6 4. Qf7+ Kg4 5. Qh5#
1. Qb7 Rh2+ 2. Nxh2 Qxh2+ 3. Bxh2 Nc6 4. Qf7+ Ke4 5. Qf4#
1. Qb7 Rh2+ 2. Nxh2 Qxh2+ 3. Bxh2 Kf6 4. Qg7+ Kf5 5. Qg6#
1. Qb7 Rh2+ 2. Nxh2 Qxh2+ 3. Bxh2 Kf6 4. Qd7 e2 5. Qxe6#
1. Qb7 Rh2+ 2. Nxh2 Qxh2+ 3. Bxh2 Kf6 4. Qd7 e5 5. Qe6#
1. Qb7 Rh2+ 2. Nxh2 Qxh2+ 3. Bxh2 Kf6 4. Qd7 e5 5. Qf7#
1. Qb7 Rh2+ 2. Nxh2 Qxh2+ 3. Bxh2 Kf6 4. Qd7 Nb5 5. Qxe6#
1. Qb7 Rh2+ 2. Nxh2 Qxh2+ 3. Bxh2 Kf6 4. Qd7 Nc8 5. Qxe6#
1. Qb7 Rh2+ 2. Nxh2 Qxh2+ 3. Bxh2 Kf6 4. Qd7 Nc6 5. Qxe6#
1. Qb7 Rh2+ 2. Nxh2 Qxh2+ 3. Bxh2 Kf6 4. Qd7 Kf5 5. Qxe6#
1. Qb7 Rh2+ 2. Nxh2 Qxh2+ 3. Bxh2 Kg4 4. Bxe6+ Kh4 5. Qe4#
1. Qb7 Rh2+ 2. Nxh2 Qxh2+ 3. Bxh2 Kg4 4. Bxe6+ Kh4 5. Qb4#
1. Qb7 Rh2+ 2. Nxh2 Qxh2+ 3. Bxh2 Kg4 4. Bxe6+ Kh4 5. Qe7#
1. Qb7 Rh2+ 2. Nxh2 Qxh2+ 3. Bxh2 Kg4 4. Qg2+ Kh4 5. Qg3#
1. Qb7 Rh2+ 2. Nxh2 Qxh2+ 3. Bxh2 Kg4 4. Qg2+ Kf5 5. Qf3#
1. Qb7 Rh2+ 2. Nxh2 Qxh2+ 3. Bxh2 Kg4 4. Qg2+ Kf5 5. Qg6#

CGCP 01091

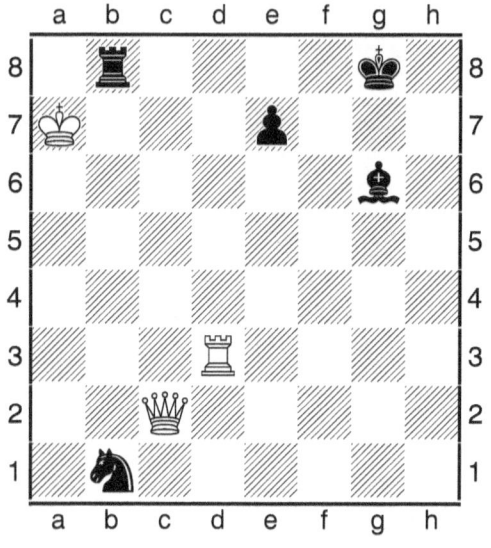

1. Rg3 Ra8+ 2. Kxa8 e6 3. Qxg6+ Kf8 4. Qh7 Nc3 5. Rg8#

1. Rg3 Ra8+ 2. Kxa8 e5 3. Qf5 e4 4. Rxg6+ Kh8 5. Qh5#

1. Rg3 Ra8+ 2. Kxa8 e5 3. Qf5 e4 4. Rxg6+ Kh8 5. Qh3#

1. Rg3 Ra8+ 2. Kxa8 e5 3. Qf5 Kh8 4. Qxg6 e4 5. Rh3#

1. Rg3 Ra8+ 2. Kxa8 e5 3. Qf5 Kh8 4. Qxg6 e4 5. Qg8#

1. Rg3 Ra8+ 2. Kxa8 e5 3. Qf5 Kh8 4. Qxg6 e4 5. Qh6#

1. Rg3 Ra8+ 2. Kxa8 e5 3. Qf5 Kh8 4. Qxg6 e4 5. Qg7#

CGCP 01104

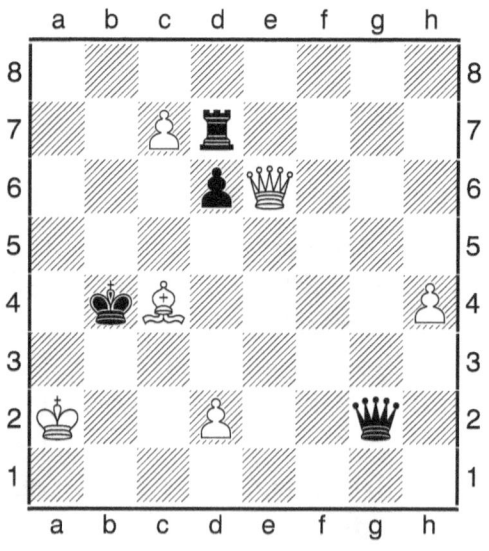

1. Qe3 Qa8+ 2. Kb2 Rxc7 {Qd5 c8=Q Rc7 Qc3 Kc5 Qxc7 Qc6 d4} 3. Qc3+ Kc5 4. Bd5+ Kxd5 5. Qf3+ Ke6 {Kc5 Qxa8 Rh7 h5 d5 h6 Kb6 Qe8} 6. Qxa8 Rf7 {d5 h5 Rg7 Qe8 Kf6 Qf8 Rf7 Qd6 Kg7} 7. h5 {Qg2 Ke7 h5 Rf8 Qb7 Ke6 h6 Rf2 Qc8} Kf6 {Rc7 Qe4 Kf6 h6} 8. Qf3+ {Kc3 Rc7 Kb2 Rg7 Qf8 Rf7 Qxd6 Kg7} Kg7 9. Qg3+ {Qxf7 Kxf7 Kc3 Kf6 Kd4 d5 h6 Kg6 Kxd5} Kh8 10. Qxd6 {h6 Rb7 Kc2 Kh7 Qd3 Kxh6 Qxd6 Kh7 Qh2} Rg7 {Rb7 Kc2 Rf7 h6 Kh7 Kb2 Rb7 Kc3} 11. Qh6+ {Qf8 Kh7 Qxg7 Kxg7 d4 Kf8 h6 Kf7} Kg8 12. d4 {Qxg7 Kxg7 d4 Kg8 d5 Kg7 d6 Kh6} Rg3 {Rb7 Kc3 Rc7 Kd3 Ra7 Qg6 Kh8 h6} 13. Qf4 {d5 Rg7 d6 Rg2 Kb3 Rg3 Kb4 Rg4 Kc5} 1-0

104

CGCP 01105

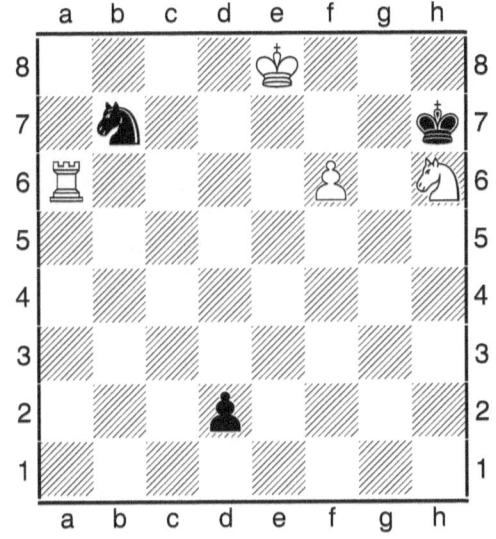

1. f7 Nd6+ 2. Rxd6 d1=Q 3. f8=N+ Kh8 4. Nf7+ Kg7 5. Rg6#
1. f7 Nd6+ 2. Rxd6 d1=Q 3. f8=N+ Kg7 4. Rg6+ Kh8 5. Rg8#
1. f7 Nd6+ 2. Rxd6 d1=Q 3. f8=N+ Kg7 4. Rg6+ Kh8 5. Nf7#
1. f7 Nd6+ 2. Rxd6 d1=B 3. Nf5 Ba4+ 4. Kf8 Bb5 5. Rh6#

CGCP 01107

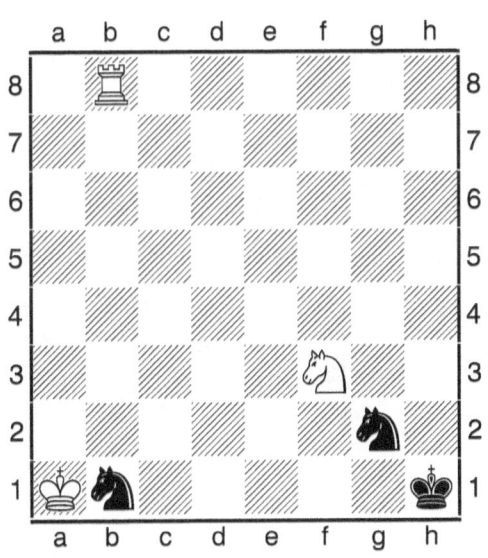

1. Rb2 Na3 2. Rf2 Nc2+ 3. Rxc2 Nh4 4. Rh2#
1. Rb2 Na3 2. Rf2 Nc2+ 3. Rxc2 Ne1 4. Rh2#
1. Rb2 Na3 2. Rf2 Nc2+ 3. Rxc2 Nf4 4. Rh2#
1. Rb2 Na3 2. Rf2 Nc2+ 3. Rxc2 Ne3 4. Rh2#
1. Rb2 Nc3 2. Rf2 Ne2 3. Rf1+ Ng1 4. Rxg1#
1. Rb2 Nc3 2. Rf2 Ne2 3. Rxe2 Ne3 4. Rh2#
1. Rb2 Nc3 2. Rf2 Ne2 3. Rxe2 Ne1 4. Rh2#
1. Rb2 Nc3 2. Rf2 Ne2 3. Rxe2 Nf4 4. Rh2#
1. Rb2 Nc3 2. Rf2 Ne2 3. Rxe2 Nh4 4. Rh2#

CGCP 01108

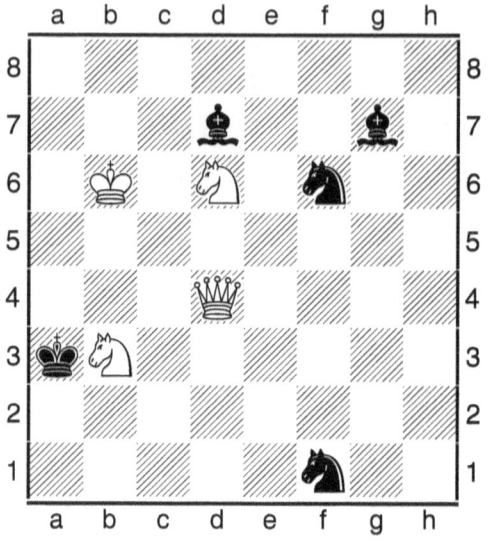

1. Nc1 Nd5+ 2. Ka5 Nd2 3. **Qxd2 Bc3+ 4. Qxc3+ Nxc3 5. Nc4#**
1. Nc1 Nd5+ 2. Ka5 Nfe3 3. Qxg7 Nf6 4. Qg2 Nc4+ 5. Nxc4#
1. Nc1 Nd5+ 2. Ka5 Nfe3 3. Qxg7 Nf6 4. Qg2 Ned5 5. Qa2#
1. Nc1 Nd5+ 2. Ka5 Nfe3 3. Qxg7 Nf6 4. Qg2 Bb5 5. Nxb5#
1. Nc1 Nd5+ 2. Ka5 Nfe3 3. Qxg7 Nf6 4. Qg2 Be6 5. Nb5#
1. Nc1 Nd5+ 2. Ka5 Nfe3 3. Qxg7 Nf6 4. Qxf6 Nc2 5. Qc3#
1. Nc1 Nd5+ 2. Ka5 Nfe3 3. Qxg7 Nf6 4. Qxf6 Nd5 5. Qa1#

CGCP 01126

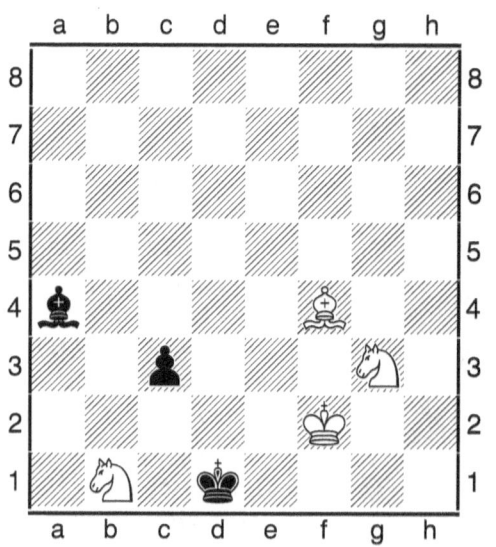

1. Na3 c2 2. Ne2 c1=Q 3. Nxc1 Bb5 4. Na2 Ba4 5. Nc3#
1. Na3 c2 2. Ne2 c1=Q 3. Nxc1 Bc6 4. Nd3 Bd7 5. Nb2#

106

CGCP 01130

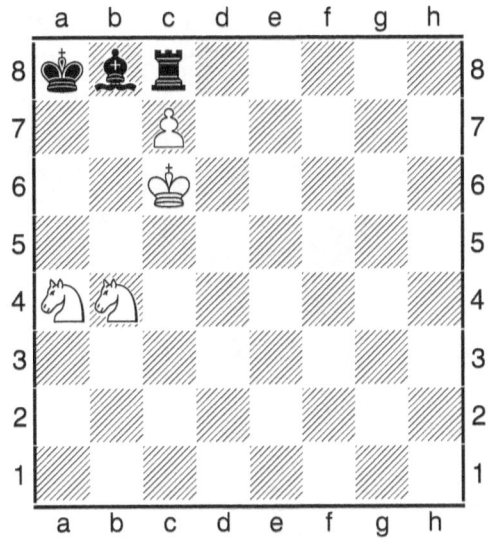

1. Nb6+ Ka7 2. Nxc8+ Ka8 3. Nb6+ Ka7 4. c8=N#

CGCP 01147

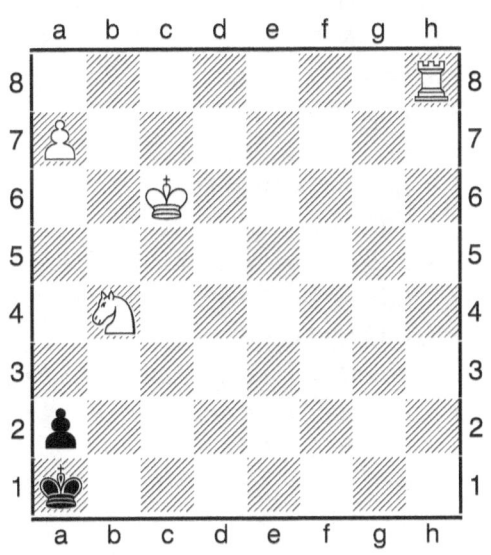

1. a8=R Kb2 2. Rxa2+ Kc3 3. Kc5 Kb3 4. Rh3#
1. a8=R Kb2 2. Rxa2+ Kb3 3. Kc5 Kc3 4. Rh3#

CGCP 01155

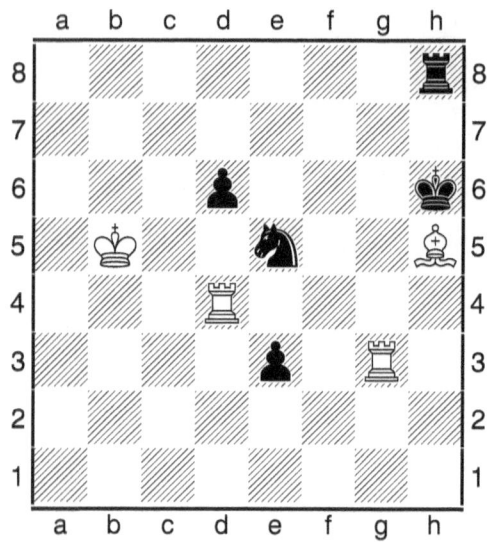

1. Be8 Nf3 2. Rxd6+ Kh7 3. Rd5 Nd4+ 4. Rxd4 Kh6 5. Rh4#
1. Be8 Nf3 2. Rxd6+ Kh7 3. Rd5 Nd4+ 4. Rxd4 Rg8 5. Rh4#
1. Be8 Nf3 2. Rxd6+ Kh7 3. Rd5 Nd4+ 4. Rxd4 Rf8 5. Rh4#
1. Be8 Nf3 2. Rxd6+ Kh7 3. Rd5 Nd4+ 4. Rxd4 Rxe8 5. Rh4#
1. Be8 Nf3 2. Rxd6+ Kh7 3. Rd5 Nd4+ 4. Rxd4 e2 5. Rh4#
1. Be8 Nf3 2. Rxd6+ Kh7 3. Rd5 Ne5 4. Rxe5 e2 5. Rh5#
1. Be8 Nf3 2. Rxd6+ Kh7 3. Rd5 Ne5 4. Rxe5 Rg8 5. Rh5#
1. Be8 Nf3 2. Rxd6+ Kh7 3. Rd5 Ne5 4. Rxe5 Rf8 5. Rh5#
1. Be8 Nf3 2. Rxd6+ Kh7 3. Rd5 Ne5 4. Rxe5 Rxe8 5. Rh5#
1. Be8 Nf3 2. Rxd6+ Kh7 3. Rd5 Ne5 4. Rxe5 Kh6 5. Rh5#
1. Be8 Nf3 2. Rxd6+ Kh7 3. Rd5 Ng5 4. Rdxg5 e2 5. Rh3#
1. Be8 Nf3 2. Rxd6+ Kh7 3. Rd5 Ng5 4. Rdxg5 e2 5. Rh5#
1. Be8 Nf3 2. Rxd6+ Kh7 3. Rd5 Ng5 4. Rdxg5 Rg8 5. Rh3#
1. Be8 Nf3 2. Rxd6+ Kh7 3. Rd5 Ng5 4. Rdxg5 Rg8 5. Rh5#
1. Be8 Nf3 2. Rxd6+ Kh7 3. Rd5 Ng5 4. Rdxg5 Rf8 5. Rh3#
1. Be8 Nf3 2. Rxd6+ Kh7 3. Rd5 Ng5 4. Rdxg5 Rf8 5. Rh5#
1. Be8 Nf3 2. Rxd6+ Kh7 3. Rd5 Ng5 4. Rdxg5 Rxe8 5. Rh3#
1. Be8 Nf3 2. Rxd6+ Kh7 3. Rd5 Ng5 4. Rdxg5 Rxe8 5. Rh5#
1. Be8 Nf3 2. Rxd6+ Kh7 3. Rd5 Ng5 4. Rdxg5 Kh6 5. Rh5#

CGCP 01157

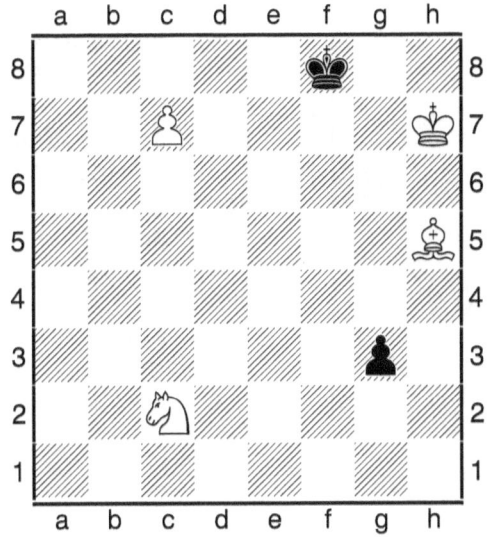

1. c8=N g2 2. Nd4 g1=Q 3. Ne6#
1. c8=N g2 2. Nd4 g1=N 3. Ne6#
1. c8=N g2 2. Nd4 g1=R 3. Ne6#
1. c8=N g2 2. Nd4 g1=B 3. Ne6#

CGCP 01170

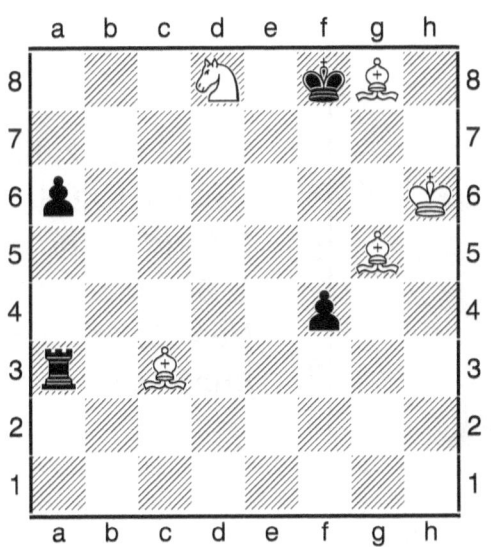

1. Bf7 Rxc3 2. Kg6 Re3 3. Kf6 Rf3 4. Ne6#
1. Bf7 Rxc3 2. Kg6 Rc6+ 3. Nxc6 f3 4. Bh6#
1. Bf7 Rxc3 2. Kg6 Rc6+ 3. Nxc6 a5 4. Be7#
1. Bf7 Rxc3 2. Kg6 Re3 3. Kf6 Re6+ 4. Nxe6#

CGCP 01173

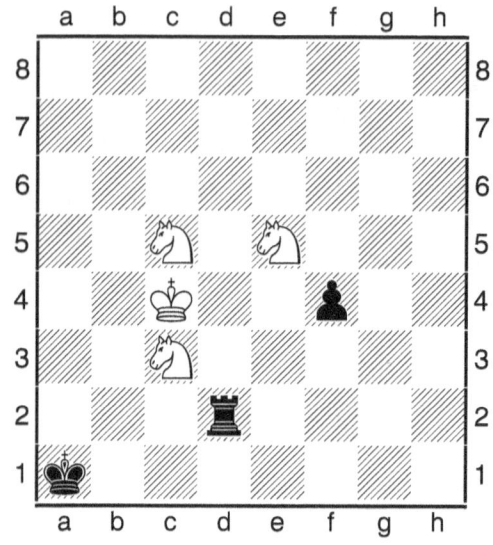

1. Ned3 Rxd3 2. Nxd3 f3 3. Kb3 f2 4. Nb4 f1=Q 5. Nc2#

1. Ned3 Rb2 2. Nb3+ Rxb3 3. Kxb3 f3 4. Ne1 f2 5. Nc2#

1. Ned3 Rb2 2. Nb3+ Rxb3 3. Kxb3 f3 4. Nb4 f2 5. Nc2#

1. Ned3 Rxd3 2. Nxd3 f3 3. Kb3 f2 4. Nb4 f1=N 5. Nc2#

1. Ned3 Rxd3 2. Nxd3 f3 3. Kb3 f2 4. Nb4 f1=R 5. Nc2#

1. Ned3 Rxd3 2. Nxd3 f3 3. Kb3 f2 4. Nb4 f1=B 5. Nc2#

CGCP 01204

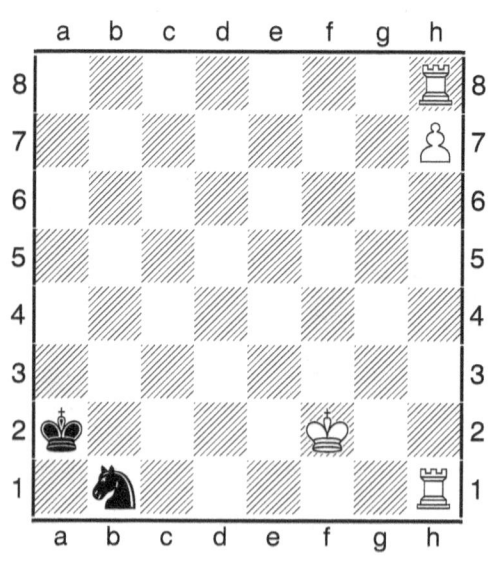

1. Rb8 Nc3 2. h8=B Ne4+ 3. Kg2 Nf6 4. Bg7 Nd7 5. Ra1#

1. Rb8 Nc3 2. h8=B Ne4+ 3. Kg2 Nf6 4. Rhb1 Ka3 5. Ra8#

CGCP 01218

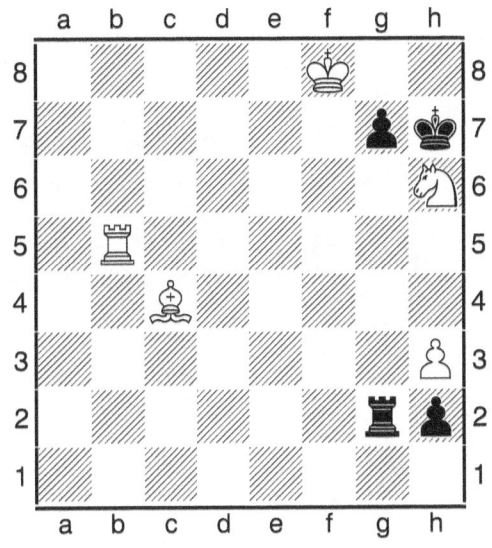

1. Rh5 Rf2+ 2. Nf5+ Kg6 3. Bf7+ Kf6 4. Nxg7 Rg2 5. Ne8#

1. Rh5 Rf2+ 2. Nf5+ Kg6 3. Bf7+ Kf6 4. Nxg7 Rg2 5. Rf5#

1. Rh5 Rf2+ 2. Nf5+ Kg6 3. Bf7+ Kf6 4. Nxg7 Rf5 5. Rxf5#

1. Rh5 gxh6 2. Bd3+ Rg6 3. Kf7 h1=Q 4. Bxg6+ Kh8 5. Rxh6#

1. Rh5 Rg5 2. Bd3+ g6 3. Rh4 h1=Q 4. Nf7+ Rh5 5. Rxh5#

1. Rh5 Rg5 2. Bd3+ g6 3. Rh4 Rh5 4. Rxh5 h1=Q 5. Nf7#

1. Rh5 Rg5 2. Bd3+ g6 3. Rh4 Rh5 4. Rxh5 h1=Q 5. Ng8#

1. Rh5 Rg5 2. Bd3+ g6 3. Rh4 Rh5 4. Rxh5 h1=Q 5. Ng4#

CGCP 01221

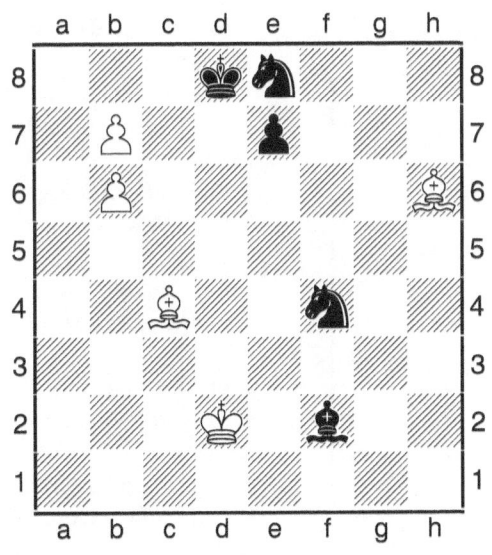

1. Bb5 Be1+ 2. Kc2 e6 3. Bg5+ Nf6 4. Bxf6#

1. Bb5 Be1+ 2. Kc2 Nd6 3. b8=Q+ Nc8 4. Qc7#

CGCP 01224

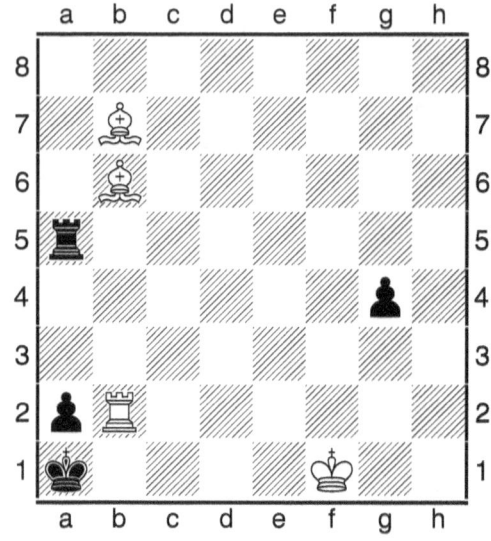

1. Bd4 Rf5+ 2. Rf2+ Kb1 3. Be4+ Kc1 4. Bb2+ Kd1 5. Bc2#
1. Bd4 Rf5+ 2. Rf2+ Kb1 3. Be4+ Kc1 4. Be3+ Kd1 5. Bc2#

CGCP 01268

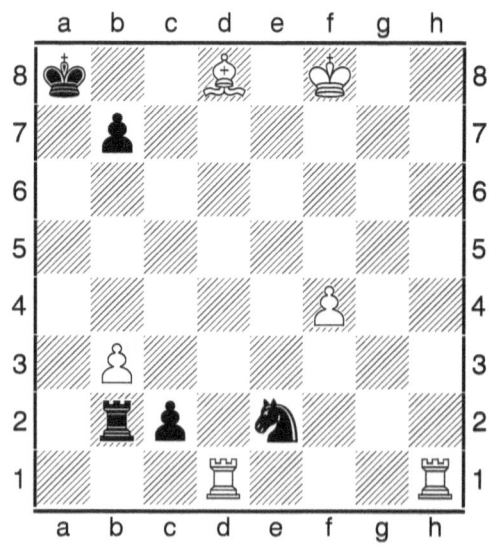

1. Bb6 cxd1=Q 2. Rxd1 Nd4 3. Rxd4 Rd2 4. Rxd2 Kb8 5. Rd8#
1. Bb6 cxd1=Q 2. Rxd1 Nd4 3. Rxd4 Rc2 4. Rd8+ Rc8 5. Rxc8#
1. Bb6 cxd1=Q 2. Rxd1 Rd2 3. Rxd2 Nd4 4. Rxd4 Kb8 5. Rd8#
1. Bb6 cxd1=R 2. Rxd1 Nd4 3. Rxd4 Rc2 4. Rd8+ Rc8 5. Rxc8#
1. Bb6 cxd1=R 2. Rxd1 Nd4 3. Rxd4 Rd2 4. Rxd2 Kb8 5. Rd8#
1. Bb6 cxd1=R 2. Rxd1 Rd2 3. Rxd2 Nd4 4. Rxd4 Kb8 5. Rd8#

CGCP 01277

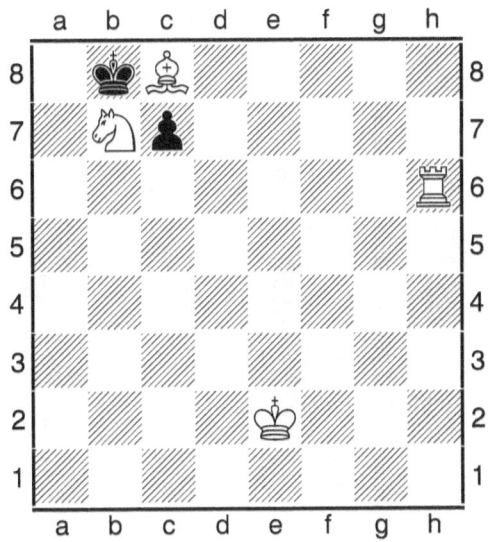

1. Nc5 c6 2. Rxc6 Ka8 3. Nd7 Ka7 4. Ra6#
1. Nc5 c6 2. Rxc6 Ka7 3. Nd7 Ka8 4. Ra6#
1. Nc5 Ka8 2. Nd7 c6 3. Rxc6 Ka7 4. Ra6#
1. Nc5 Ka8 2. Nd7 c6 3. Rh4 c5 4. Ra4#
1. Nc5 Ka8 2. Nd7 c6 3. Rh4 Ka7 4. Ra4#
1. Nc5 Ka8 2. Nd7 c6 3. Rh3 c5 4. Ra3#
1. Nc5 Ka8 2. Nd7 c6 3. Rh3 Ka7 4. Ra3#
1. Nc5 Ka8 2. Nd7 c6 3. Rh1 c5 4. Ra1#
1. Nc5 Ka8 2. Nd7 c6 3. Rh1 Ka7 4. Ra1#
1. Nc5 Ka7 2. Nd7 c6 3. Rxc6 Ka8 4. Ra6#
1. Nc5 Ka7 2. Nd7 c6 3. Rh4 c5 4. Ra4#
1. Nc5 Ka7 2. Nd7 c6 3. Rh4 Ka8 4. Ra4#
1. Nc5 Ka7 2. Nd7 c6 3. Rh3 c5 4. Ra3#
1. Nc5 Ka7 2. Nd7 c6 3. Rh3 Ka8 4. Ra3#
1. Nc5 Ka7 2. Nd7 c6 3. Rh1 c5 4. Ra1#
1. Nc5 Ka7 2. Nd7 c6 3. Rh1 Ka8 4. Ra1#

CGCP 01279

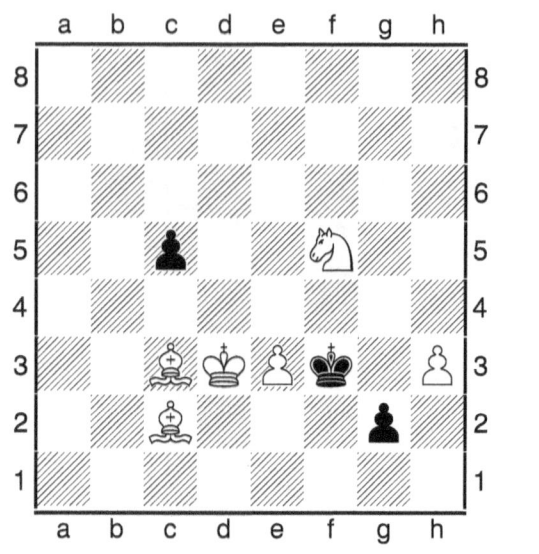

1. Be1 c4+ 2. Kd2 c3+ 3. Kd3 g1=Q 4. Nh4#

1. Be1 c4+ 2. Kd2 c3+ 3. Kd3 g1=N 4. Nh4#

1. Be1 c4+ 2. Kd2 c3+ 3. Kd3 g1=R 4. Nh4#

1. Be1 c4+ 2. Kd2 c3+ 3. Kd3 g1=B 4. Nh4#

CGCP 01285

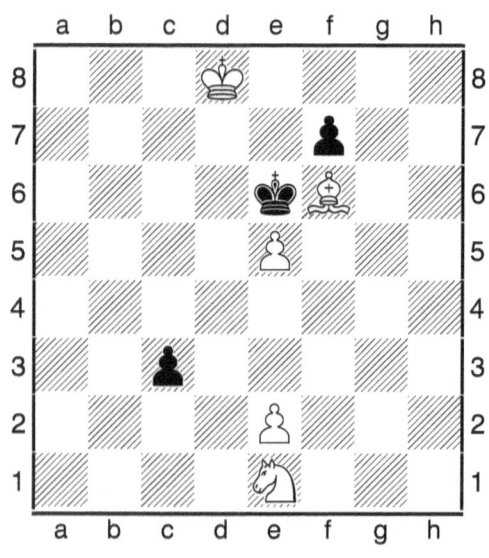

1. e4 c2 2. Nf3 c1=Q 3. Nd4#

1. e4 c2 2. Nf3 c1=N 3. Nd4#

1. e4 c2 2. Nf3 c1=N 3. Ng5#

1. e4 c2 2. Nf3 c1=R 3. Nd4#

1. e4 c2 2. Nf3 c1=R 3. Ng5#

1. e4 c2 2. Nf3 c1=B 3. Nd4#

114

CGCP 01289

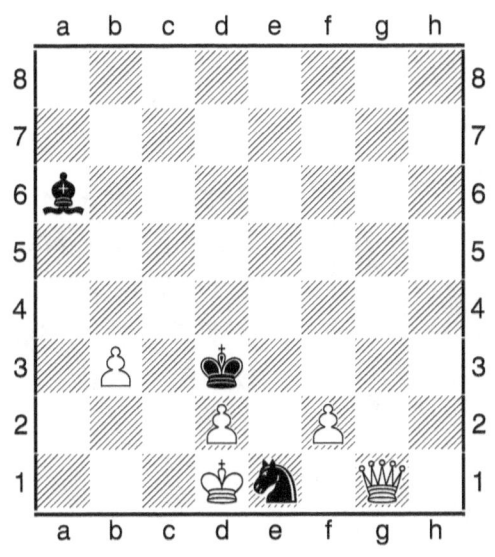

**1. f3 Nc2 2. Qg6+ Kd4
3. Qd6#**
1. f3 Nc2 2. Qc5 Ne3+
3. Qxe3#
1. f3 Nc2 2. Qc5 Na3
3. Qe3#
1. f3 Nc2 2. Qc5 Na3
3. Qc3#
1. f3 Nc2 2. Qc5 Na3
3. Qd5#
1. f3 Nc2 2. Qc5 Bb7
3. Qc4#
1. f3 Nc2 2. Qc5 Bc4
3. Qxc4#

CGCP 01297

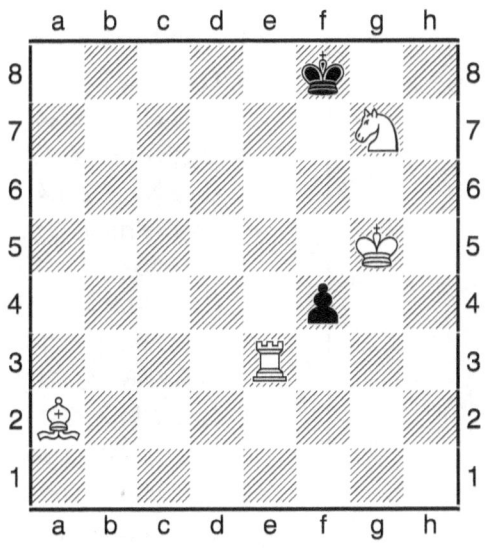

**1. Kf6 fxe3 2. Bf7
e2 3. Ne6#**

115

CGCP 01300

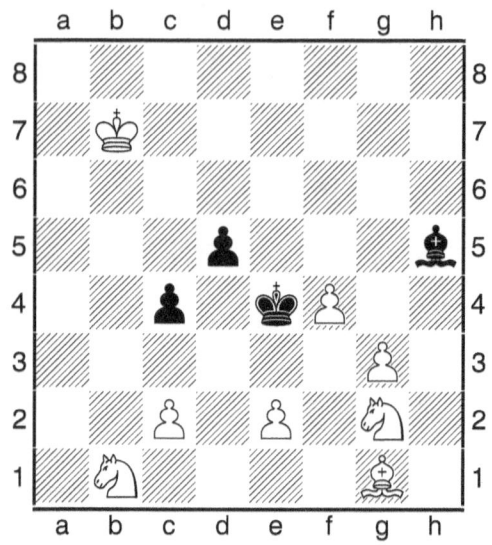

1. Nh4 d4 2. Kc6 Be8+ 3. Kc5 c3 4. Bxd4 Bb5 5. Nxc3#
1. Nh4 d4 2. Kc6 c3 3. Kc5 Bg4 4. Bxd4 Bf3 5. exf3#

CGCP 01307

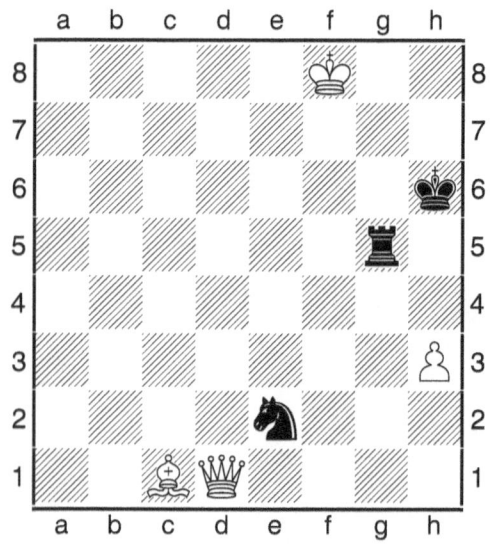

1. Qd2 Nxc1 2. h4 Kh7 3. Qxg5 Na2 4. Qg7#
1. Qd2 Nxc1 2. h4 Nb3 3. Qxg5+ Kh7 4. Qh5#
1. Qd2 Nxc1 2. h4 Kh7 3. Qxg5 Kh8 4. Qg8#
1. Qd2 Nxc1 2. h4 Kh7 3. Qxg5 Kh8 4. Qh6#
1. Qd2 Nf4 2. Qxf4 Kg6 3. Kg8 Kh6+ 4. Qxg5#
1. Qd2 Nf4 2. Qxf4 Kg6 3. Kg8 Rh5 4. Qf7#
1. Qd2 Nf4 2. Qxf4 Kh7 3. Qxg5 Kh8 4. Qh4#

CGCP 01309

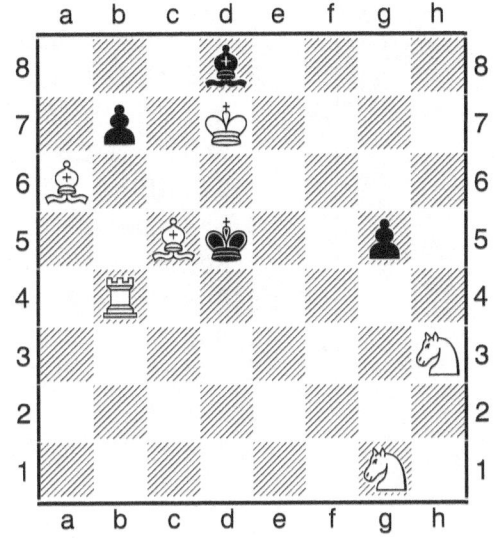

**1. Bd6 bxa6 2. Nf4+
gxf4 3. Ne2 a5 4. Nc3#**
1. Bd6 bxa6 2. Nf4+
gxf4 3. Ne2 f3 4. Nf4#
1. Bd6 bxa6 2. Nf4+
gxf4 3. Ne2 f3 4. Rd4#
1. Bd6 bxa6 2. Nf4+
gxf4 3. Ne2 a5 4. Nxf4#

CGCP 01314

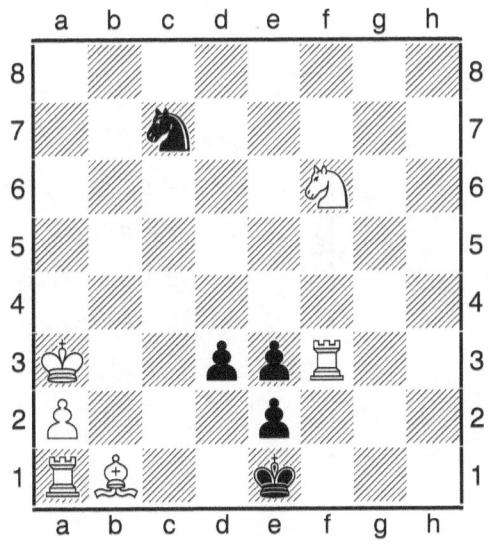

**1. Ne4 Nb5+ 2. Kb4 d2
3. Bd3+ d1=Q 4. Rg3
Qxa1 5. Rg1#**
1. Ne4 Nb5+ 2. Kb4 d2
3. Bd3+ d1=Q 4. Rg3
Qc1 5. Rxc1#
1. Ne4 Nb5+ 2. Kb4 d2
3. Bd3+ d1=Q 4. Rg3
Qb1+ 5. Rxb1#
1. Ne4 Nb5+ 2. Kb4 d2
3. Bd3+ d1=Q 4. Rg3
Kf1 5. Rxd1#

CGCP 01326

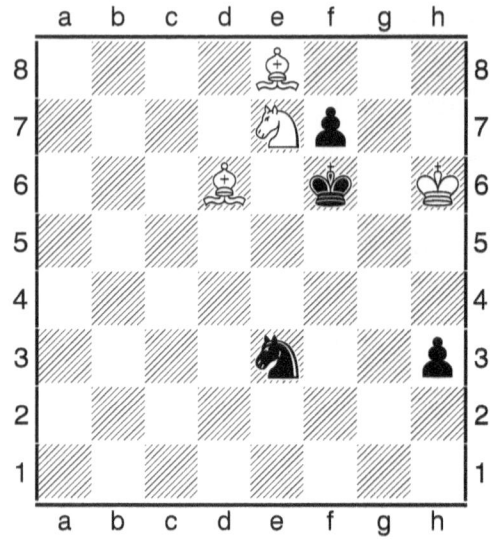

1. Bd7 Nf5+ 2. Bxf5 h2
3. Bh3 h1=Q 4. Ng8#
1. Bd7 Nf5+ 2. Bxf5 h2
3. Bh3 h1=N 4. Nd5#
1. Bd7 Nf5+ 2. Bxf5 h2
3. Bh3 h1=N 4. Ng8#
1. Bd7 Nf5+ 2. Bxf5 h2
3. Bh3 h1=R 4. Nd5#
1. Bd7 Nf5+ 2. Bxf5 h2
3. Bh3 h1=R 4. Ng8#
1. Bd7 Nf5+ 2. Bxf5 h2
3. Bh3 h1=B 4. Ng8#

CGCP 01356

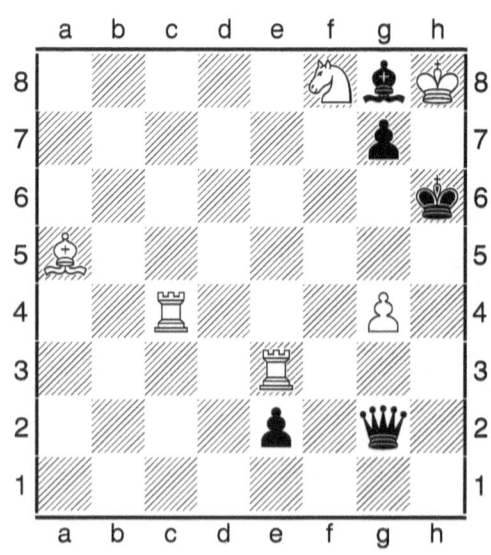

1. Bd2 g5 2. Rc6+
Qxc6 3. Rh3#
1. Bd2 g5 2. Rc6+
Be6 3. Rcxe6#
1. Bd2 g5 2. Rc6+
Be6 3. Rexe6#
1. Bd2 Kg5 2. Rf3+
Kh4 3. Ng6#

CGCP 01366

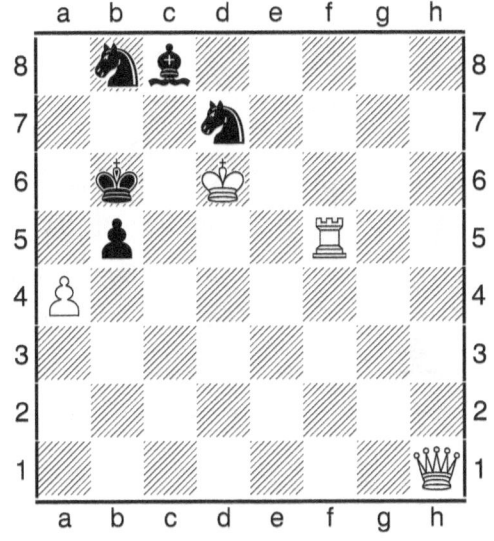

1. Qa8 bxa4 2. Qa5+ Kb7 3. Rb5+ Nb6 4. Rxb6#

CGCP 01372

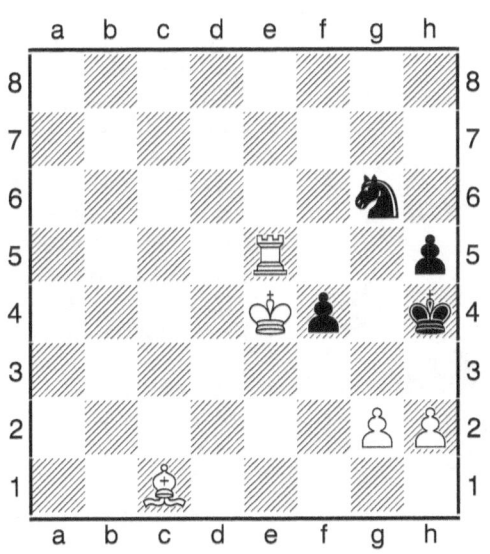

1. Kf5 Nxe5 2. Bxf4 Nc6 3. Bg5#
1. Kf5 Ne7+ 2. Rxe7 f3 3. Re4#
1. Kf5 Nxe5 2. Bxf4 Nc6 3. Bg3#
1. Kf5 Nf8 2. Bd2 Nd7 3. Be1#
1. Kf5 Nf8 2. Be3 f3 3. Bf2#

CGCP 01406

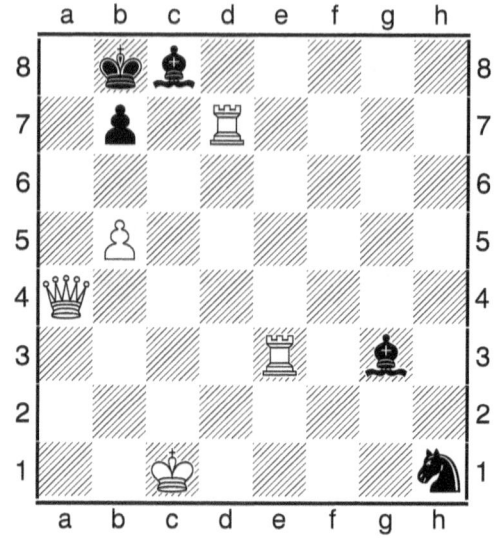

1. b6 Bxd7 2. Re8+ Bxe8 3. Qxe8#
1. b6 Bxd7 2. Re8+ Bc8 3. Qa7#

CGCP 01414

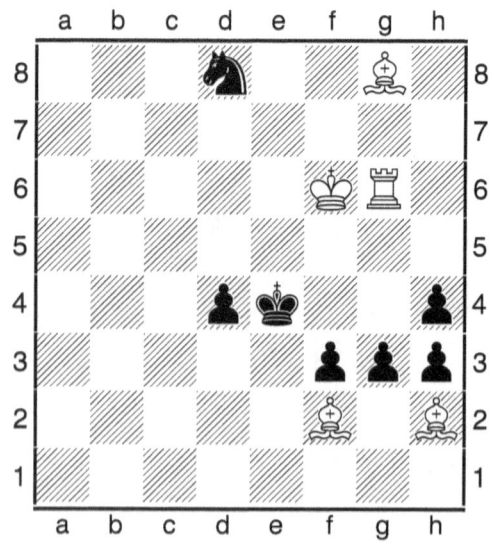

1. Bc4 Ne6 2. Kxe6 gxf2 3. Rg4+ Ke3 4. Bf4+ Ke4 5. Bh6#
1. Bc4 Ne6 2. Kxe6 gxf2 3. Rg4+ Ke3 4. Bf4+ Ke4 5. Bd2#
1. Bc4 Ne6 2. Kxe6 gxf2 3. Rg4+ Ke3 4. Bf4+ Ke4 5. Bg5#
1. Bc4 Ne6 2. Kxe6 Kf4 3. Bd3 gxh2 4. Bf5 h1=Q 5. Rg4#
1. Bc4 Ne6 2. Kxe6 Kf4 3. Kf6 gxh2 4. Rh6 h1=Q 5. Rxh4#
1. Bc4 Kf4 2. Rh6 Kg4 3. Bxd4 g2 4. Bd3 g1=Q 5. Bf5#
1. Bc4 Kf4 2. Rh6 Kg4 3. Bxd4 g2 4. Bd3 f2 5. Be2#
1. Bc4 Kf4 2. Rh6 Kg4 3. Bxd4 g2 4. Bf2 Nb7 5. Be6#
1. Bc4 Kf4 2. Rh6 Kg4 3. Bxd4 g2 4. Bf2 Ne6 5. Bxe6#

CGCP 01419

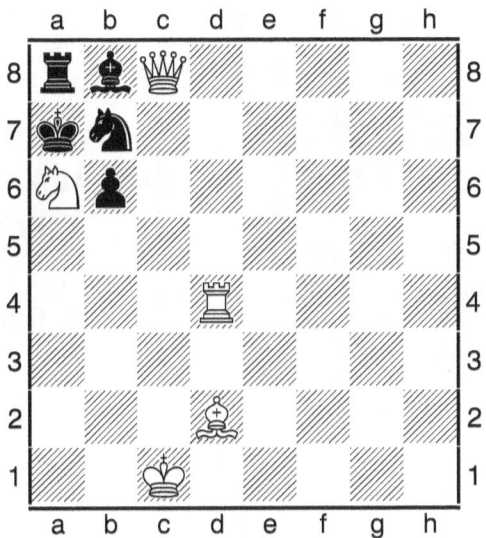

1. Ra4 Na5 2. Nb4 Be5 3. Nc6#
1. Ra4 b5 2. Nc5+ Na5 3. Qa6#
1. Ra4 b5 2. Nc5+ bxa4 3. Qxb7#
1. Ra4 b5 2. Nc5+ Kb6 3. Nd7#
1. Ra4 b5 2. Be3+ Nc5 3. Bxc5#
1. Ra4 Na5 2. Nb4 b5 3. Be3#
1. Ra4 Na5 2. Nb4 Bc7 3. Qxc7#
1. Ra4 b5 2. Nc5+ Na5 3. Qb7#
1. Ra4 Bc7 2. Nxc7+ Na5 3. Nb5#
1. Ra4 Bc7 2. Nxc7+ Na5 3. Qxa8#
1. Ra4 Bc7 2. Qxc7 Rb8 3. Nxb8#
1. Ra4 Bc7 2. Qxc7 Rb8 3. Nb4#
1. Ra4 Bc7 2. Qxc7 Rb8 3. Nc5#
1. Ra4 Bc7 2. Qxc7 Rb8 3. Qxb8#
1. Ra4 Bc7 2. Qxc7 Rc8 3. Nb8#

CGCP 01429

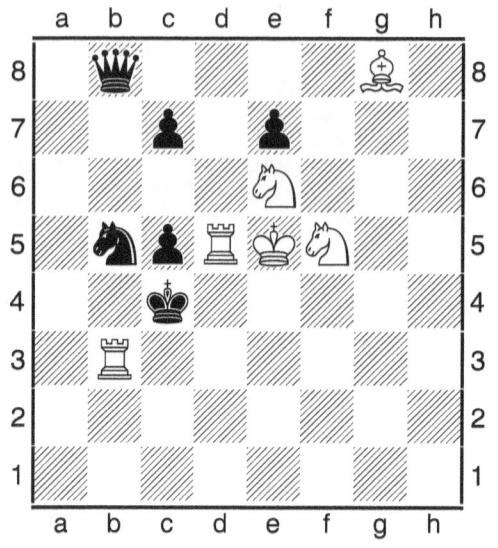

1. Rdd3 c6+ 2. Nc7+ Qxg8 3. Ne3#
1. Rdd3 c6+ 2. Nc7+ e6 3. Bxe6#
1. Rdd3 c6+ 2. Nc7+ e6 3. Ne3#

CGCP 01446

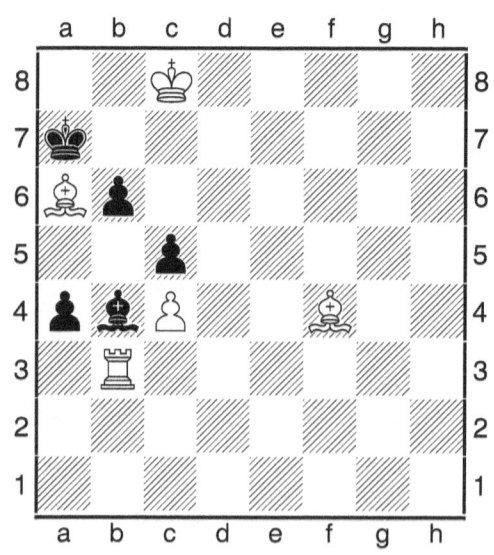

1. Bb5 axb3 2. Bb8+ Ka8 3. Bc6#
1. Bb5 Ba3 2. Rxa3 Ka8 3. Rxa4#

CGCP 01455

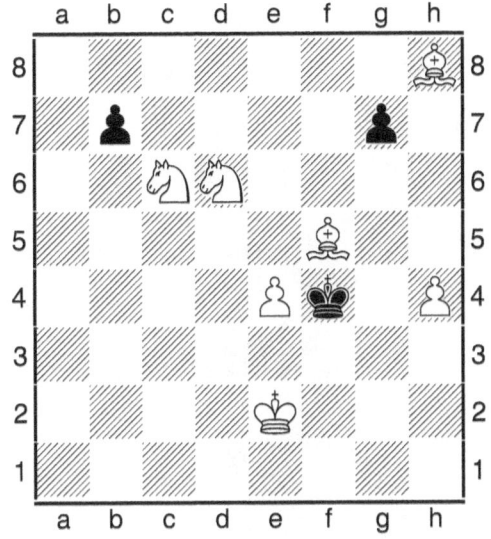

1. Kf2 bxc6 2. Nc4 c5 3. Kg2 g6 4. Be5#
1. Kf2 bxc6 2. Nc4 c5 3. Kg2 g5 4. Be5#
1. Kf2 bxc6 2. Nf7 c5 3. Bxg7 c4 4. Bh6#
1. Kf2 bxc6 2. Nf7 c5 3. Bxg7 c4 4. Be5#
1. Kf2 bxc6 2. Bxg7 c5 3. Nf7 c4 4. Bh6#
1. Kf2 bxc6 2. Bxg7 c5 3. Nf7 c4 4. Be5#

CGCP 01462

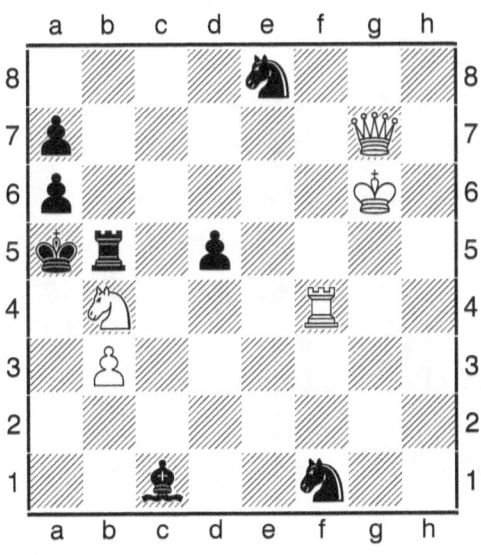

1. Qc3 Bd2 2. Nxd5+ Rb4 3. Qc5+ Rb5 4. Ra4#
1. Qc3 Bd2 2. Nxd5+ Rb4 3. Qc5+ Rb5 4. Qa3#
1. Qc3 Ba3 2. Nxd5+ Rb4 3. Rxb4 Nd2 4. Qc5#
1. Qc3 Ba3 2. Nxd5+ Rb4 3. Rxb4 Nc7 4. Qxc7#
1. Qc3 Ba3 2. Nxd5+ Rb4 3. Rxb4 Bxb4 4. Qxb4#
1. Qc3 Ba3 2. Nxd5+ Rb4 3. Rxb4 Bc1 4. Rb6#
1. Qc3 Ba3 2. Nxd5+ Rb4 3. Rxb4 Bc1 4. Rb7#
1. Qc3 Ba3 2. Nxd5+ Rb4 3. Rxb4 Bc1 4. Rb8#
1. Qc3 Ba3 2. Nxd5+ Bb4 3. Rxb4 Nd2 4. Qa1#
1. Qc3 Ba3 2. Nxd5+ Bb4 3. Rxb4 Rc5 4. Qxc5#

CGCP 01468

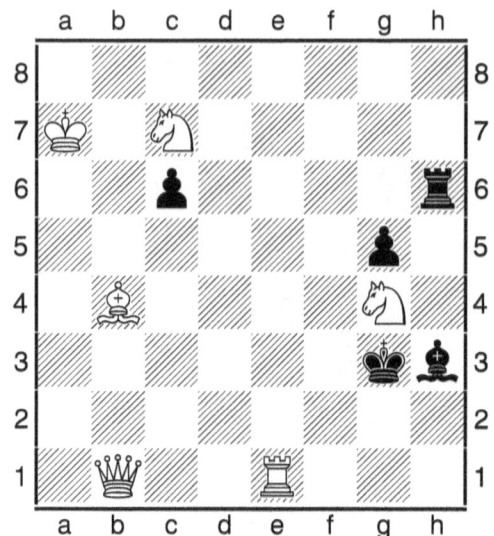

1. Qe4 Bg2 2. Re3+ Kh4 3. Nf6+ Bxe4 4. Be1#
1. Qe4 Bg2 2. Re3+ Bf3 3. Qxf3+ Kh4 4. Qh3#
1. Qe4 Bg2 2. Re3+ Kh4 3. Nf6+ g4 4. Qxg4#
1. Qe4 c5 2. Re3+ Kh4 3. Be1+ Kh5 4. Rxh3#
1. Qe4 Bf1 2. Re3+ Kh4 3. Ne5+ Kh5 4. Qg4#
1. Qe4 Rg6 2. Rh1 Rf6 3. Be1+ Rf2 4. Bxf2#
1. Qe4 Rg6 2. Rh1 Kh4 3. Qf3 c5 4. Qxh3#
1. Qe4 Rf6 2. Rg1+ Bg2 3. Qxg2+ Kh4 4. Rh1#
1. Qe4 Rf6 2. Rg1+ Bg2 3. Qxg2+ Kh4 4. Qh2#
1. Qe4 Rf6 2. Rg1+ Bg2 3. Qxg2+ Kh4 4. Qh1#
1. Qe4 Rf6 2. Rg1+ Bg2 3. Qxg2+ Kf4 4. Rf1#
1. Qe4 Rf6 2. Rg1+ Kh4 3. Qh7+ Rh6 4. Qxh6#
1. Qe4 Re6 2. Rg1+ Bg2 3. Be1+ Kh3 4. Qxg2#
1. Qe4 Rh7 2. Rg1+ Bg2 3. Rxg2+ Kh3 4. Nf2#
1. Qe4 Rh7 2. Rg1+ Bg2 3. Rxg2+ Kh4 4. Qxh7#

124

CGCP 01471

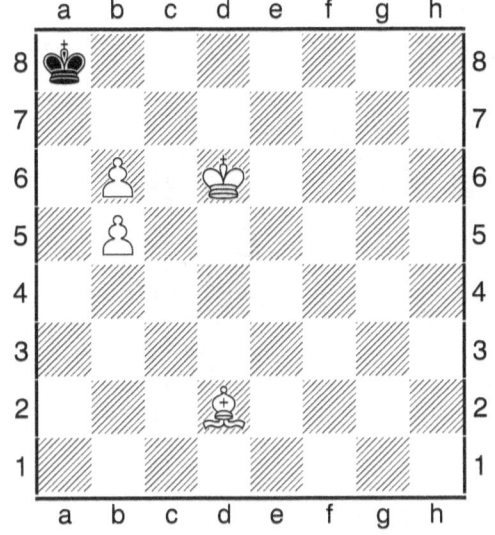

1. Kc6 Kb8 2. b7 Ka7 3. b6+ Ka6 4. b8=N#
1. Kc6 Kb8 2. b7 Ka7 3. b6+ Kb8 4. Bf4#

CGCP 01501

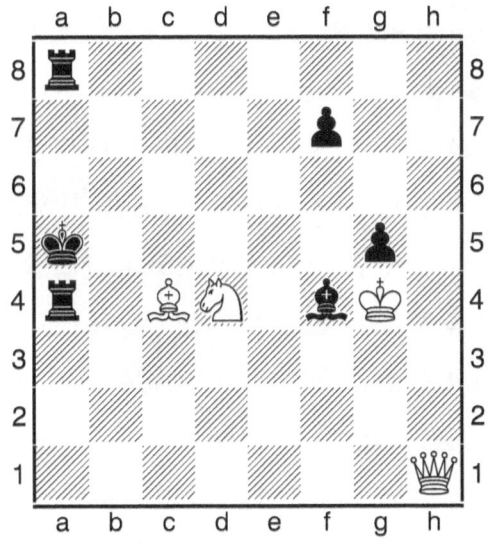

1. Qb7 f5+ 2. Kxf5 Rf8+ 3. Kg4 Bg3 4. Nc6#
1. Qb7 f5+ 2. Kxf5 Rf8+ 3. Kg4 Be3 4. Qb5#
1. Qb7 f5+ 2. Kxf5 Rf8+ 3. Kg4 Bd2 4. Nb3#
1. Qb7 f5+ 2. Kxf5 Rf8+ 3. Kg4 Rb4 4. Qa6#
1. Qb7 f5+ 2. Kxf5 Rf8+ 3. Kg4 Rb4 4. Qa7#
1. Qb7 f5+ 2. Kxf5 Rb4 3. Nc6+ Ka4 4. Qxb4#
1. Qb7 f5+ 2. Kxf5 Rb4 3. Nc6+ Ka4 4. Qxa8#

CGCP 01508

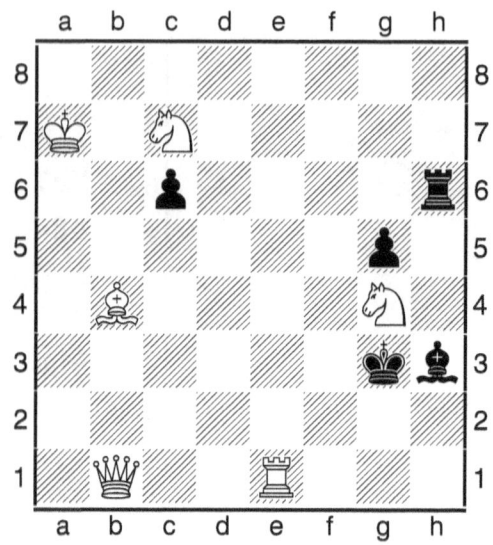

1. Re2 Rf5+ 2. Bxf5 Qxf5+ 3. Bc5+ Qxc5+ 4. Rxc5 Bb4 5. Rc4#

1. Re2 Rf5+ 2. Bxf5 Qxf5+ 3. Bc5+ Qxc5+ 4. Rxc5 e5 5. Rd5#

1. Re2 Qh5+ 2. Nxh5 Rf5+ 3. Rc5 Rxc5+ 4. Bxc5+ Kd5 5. Nf4#

1. Re2 Qh5+ 2. Nxh5 Rf5+ 3. Rc5 Rxc5+ 4. Bxc5+ Kd5 5. Ba2#

1. Re2 Qh5+ 2. Nxh5 Bxb4 3. Re4+ Kd5 4. Nxf6+ Kd6 5. Rd7#

1. Re2 Qh5+ 2. Nxh5 Bxb4 3. Re4+ Kd5 4. Rd7+ Bd6 5. Nxf6#

1. Re2 Qh5+ 2. Nxh5 Bxb4 3. Rd7+ Bd6 4. Rxd6+ Kc3 5. Rd3#

1. Re2 Qh5+ 2. Nxh5 Bxb4 3. Nxf6 Bc5 4. Rxc5 h1=N 5. Re4#

1. Re2 Qh5+ 2. Nxh5 Bxb4 3. Kxb4 e5 4. Rd7+ Rd6 5. Rxd6#

1. Re2 Qh5+ 2. Nxh5 Bxb4 3. Kxb4 e5 4. Nxf6 e4 5. Rxe4#

1. Re2 Qh5+ 2. Nxh5 Bxb4 3. Kxb4 Rf7 4. Nf6 Rd7 5. Rxd7#

1. Re2 Qh5+ 2. Nxh5 Bxb4 3. Kxb4 Kd5 4. Rd2+ Ke5 5. Rc5#

CGCP 01514

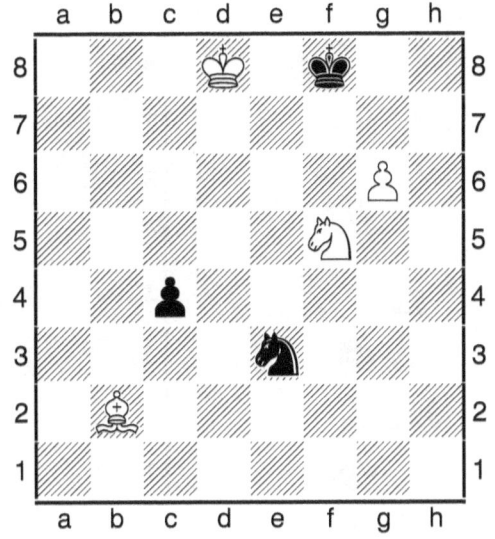

1. Nh6 c3 2. Bxc3 Nf5 3. g7+ Nxg7 4. Bb4#

CGCP 01524

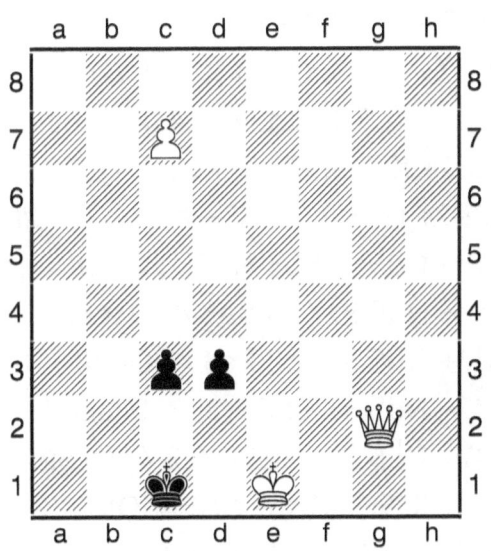

1. c8=R d2+ 2. Qxd2+ Kb1 3. Rxc3 Ka1 4. Rc1#
1. c8=R Kb1 2. Rxc3 d2+ 3. Qxd2 Ka1 4. Rc1#

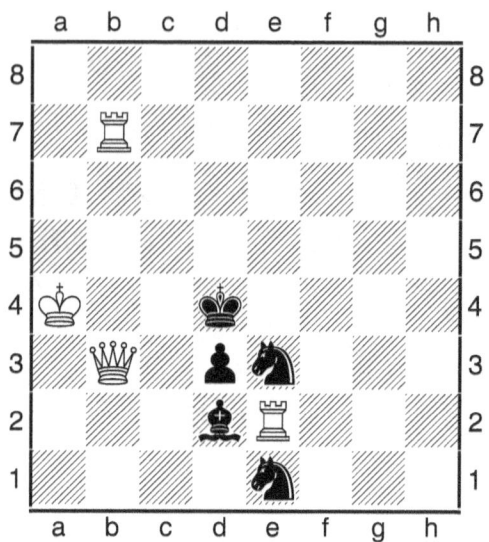

1. Qe6 dxe2 2. Rd7+ Nd5 3. Kb3 Ng2 4. Rxd5#
1. Qe6 dxe2 2. Rd7+ Nd5 3. Kb3 Be3 4. Qxd5#
1. Qe6 dxe2 2. Rd7+ Kc5 3. Qd6+ Kc4 4. Rc7#
1. Qe6 dxe2 2. Rd7+ Kc5 3. Qd6+ Kc4 4. Qd4#
1. Qe6 dxe2 2. Rd7+ Kc5 3. Qd6+ Kc4 4. Qc6#
1. Qe6 dxe2 2. Rd7+ Kc5 3. Qd6+ Kc4 4. Qc7#
1. Qe6 N1c2 2. Rd7+ Nd5 3. Qxd5+ Kc3 4. Qb3#
1. Qe6 Nf3 2. Rd7+ Nd5 3. Kb3 Ne5 4. Qb6#
1. Qe6 Nf3 2. Rd7+ Nd5 3. Kb3 Be3 4. Qxe3#
1. Qe6 Nf3 2. Rd7+ Nd5 3. Kb3 Be1 4. Qe3#
1. Qe6 Bc1 2. Rd7+ Nd5 3. Rxd5+ Kc3 4. Qc8#
1. Qe6 Bc1 2. Rd7+ Nd5 3. Qxd5+ Kc3 4. Qc5#
1. Qe6 Bc1 2. Rd7+ Kc5 3. Qd6+ Kc4 4. Qb4#
1. Qe6 Bc1 2. Rd7+ Kc5 3. Qe7+ Kc6 4. Qd6#
1. Qe6 Bc1 2. Rb4+ Kc5 3. Rxe3 d2 4. Re5#

1. Qe6 Bc1 2. Rb4+ Kc5 3. Rxe3 d2 4. Rc3#
1. Qe6 Bc1 2. Rb4+ Kc5 3. Rxe3 d2 4. Rc4#
1. Qe6 Bc3 2. Qxe3+ Kd5 3. Kb5 d2 4. Rd7#
1. Qe6 Bc3 2. Qxe3+ Kd5 3. Kb5 Bd4 4. Qe6#
1. Qe6 Bc3 2. Qxe3+ Kd5 3. Kb5 Be5 4. Qxe5#
1. Qe6 Bc3 2. Qxe3+ Kd5 3. Kb5 Bd2 4. Qe5#
1. Qe6 Bc3 2. Rxe3 d2 3. Rd7+ Kc5 4. Rxc3#
1. Qe6 Bc3 2. Rxe3 d2 3. Kb5 d1=Q 4. Qe4#
1. Qe6 Bc3 2. Rxe3 d2 3. Kb5 Nd3 4. Re4#
1. Qe6 Bc3 2. Rxe3 Nc2 3. Re4+ Kc5 4. Rb5#
1. Qe6 Bc3 2. Rxe3 Bb2 3. Qe5+ Kc4 4. Rb4#
1. Qe6 Bc3 2. Rxe3 Bd2 3. Re4+ Kc3 4. Qc4#
1. Qe6 Bc3 2. Rxe3 Bb4 3. Qe5+ Kc4 4. Rxb4#
1. Qe6 Ba5 2. Rd7+ Nd5 3. Kb3 Bb6 4. Qxb6#
1. Qe6 Kc3 2. Qe5+ Kc2 3. Qb2+ Kd1 4. Rxd2#
1. Qe6 Kc3 2. Qe5+ Kc2 3. Qb2+ Kd1 4. Qxd2#
1. Qe6 Kc3 2. Rb4 Kc2 3. Qb3+ Kc1 4. Qb1#
1. Qe6 Kc3 2. Rb4 Kc2 3. Qa2+ Kc3 4. Qb2#
1. Qe6 Kc3 2. Rb4 Kc2 3. Qa2+ Kc1 4. Rb1#
1. Qe6 Kc5 2. Rb5+ Kd4 3. Qe5+ Kc4 4. Rc5#
1. Qe6 Kc5 2. Rxe3 Ng2 3. Rxd3 Ne1 4. Qd5#
1. Qe6 Kc5 2. Rxe3 Ba5 3. Re4 Bc7 4. Rxc7#
1. Qe6 Kc5 2. Rd7 Nd5 3. Qxd5+ Kb6 4. Re6#
1. Qe6 Kc5 2. Rd7 Nd5 3. Qxd5+ Kb6 4. Qb5#
1. Qe6 Kc5 2. Rd7 Ng4 3. Rc7+ Kd4 4. Qd7#
1. Qe6 Kc5 2. Rd7 Ng4 3. Re4 Nc2 4. Rd5#
1. Qe6 Kc5 2. Rd7 Ng4 3. Re4 Ne5 4. Rxe5#
1. Qe6 Kc5 2. Rd7 Bb4 3. Qd6+ Kc4 4. Qxb4#

CGCP 01532

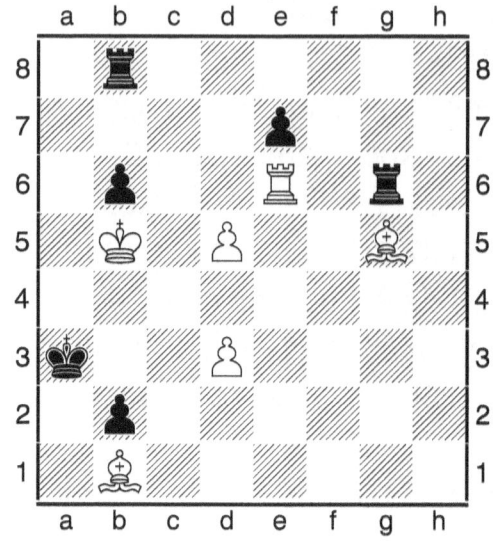

1. Re3 Re6 2. dxe6 Rc8 3. d4+ Rc3 4. Rxc3#

CGCP 01533

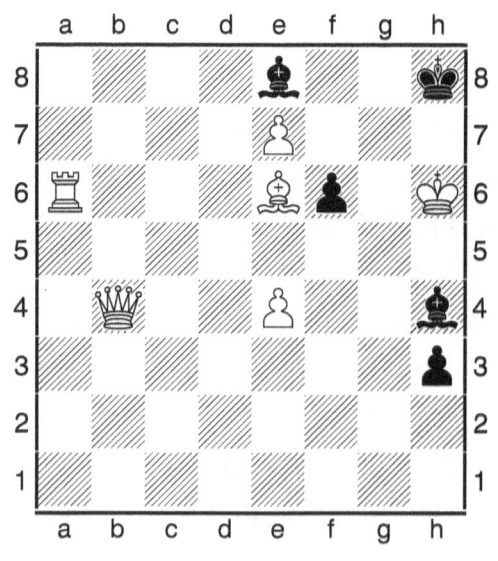

1. Qb5 Bg5+ 2. Qxg5 fxg5 3. Ra8 h2 4. Rxe8#
1. Qb5 Bg5+ 2. Qxg5 fxg5 3. Ra8 g4 4. Rxe8#

CGCP 01541

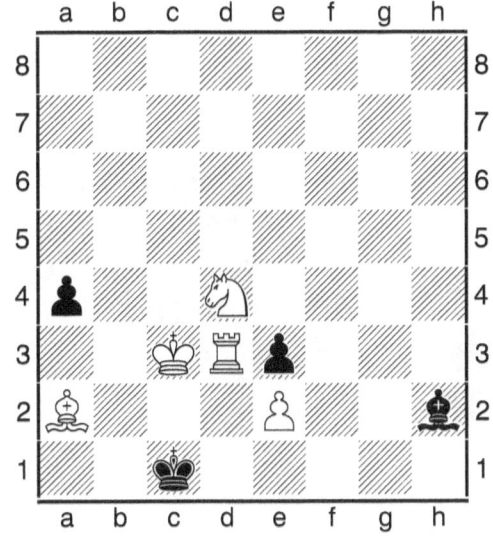

1. Bb3 axb3 2. Nxb3+ Kb1 3. Rd1+ Ka2 4. Ra1#

CGCP 01543

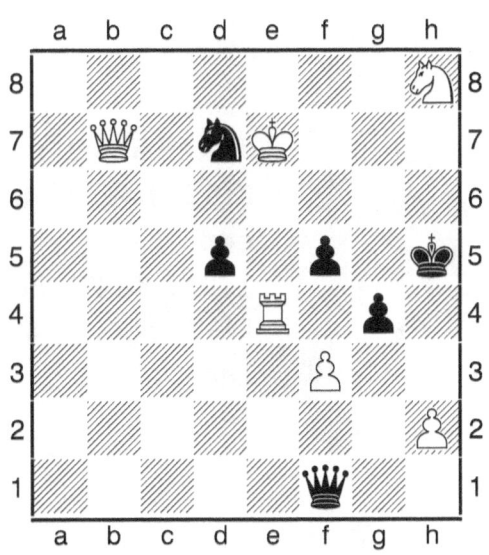

1. Qc6 Ne5 2. fxg4+ fxg4 3. Rxe5+ Qf5 4. Rxf5+ Kh4 5. Qh6#
1. Qc6 Nf8 2. Kxf8 Qc1 3. Qg6+ Kh4 4. Rxg4+ fxg4 5. Qxg4#
1. Qc6 Nf8 2. Kxf8 Qc1 3. Qg6+ Kh4 4. Rxg4+ Kh3 5. Qh5#
1. Qc6 Nf8 2. Kxf8 Qa6 3. Qxa6 d4 4. Kg7 g3 5. Qg6#
1. Qc6 Nf6 2. Qxf6 Qc1 3. fxg4+ fxg4 4. Re5+ Qg5 5. Qxg5#
1. Qc6 Nf6 2. Qxf6 Qc1 3. Qg6+ Kh4 4. Qh7+ Kg5 5. Nf7#
1. Qc6 Qa6 2. Qxa6 Nf6 3. Qxf6 d4 4. fxg4+ fxg4 5. Re5#
1. Qc6 Qa6 2. Qxa6 Nf6 3. Qxf6 d4 4. h4 gxh3ep 5. Rh4#
1. Qc6 Qa6 2. Qxa6 Nf6 3. Qxf6 d4 4. h4 gxh3ep 5. Qh4#
1. Qc6 Qa6 2. Qxa6 Nf6 3. Qxf6 d4 4. Nf7 g3 5. Qxf5#
1. Qc6 Qa6 2. Qxa6 Nf6 3. Qxf6 d4 4. Rf4 g3 5. Rxf5#
1. Qc6 Qa6 2. Qxa6 Nf6 3. Qxf6 d4 4. Rxd4 f4 5. Rd5#

CGCP 01548

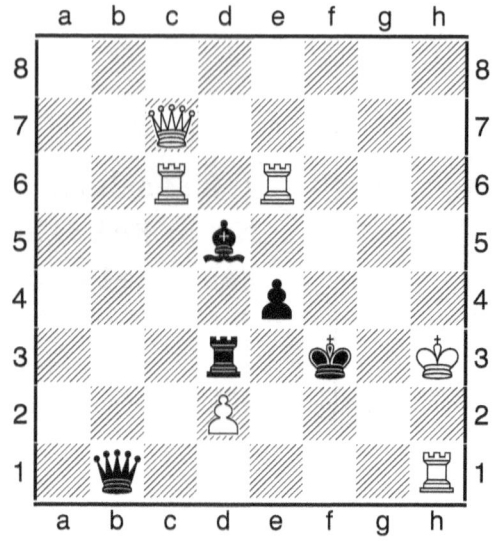

1. Qh2 Bxe6+ 2. Rxe6 Rxd2 3. Qg3+ Ke2 4. Rxe4+ Qxe4 5. Re1#

CGCP 01552

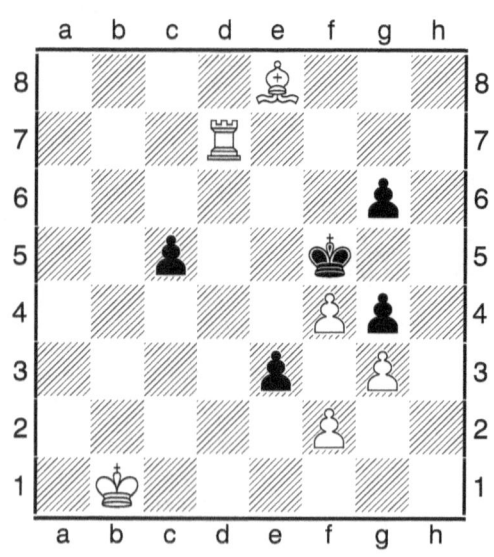

1. Rd6 Ke4 2. Bc6+ Kf5 3. fxe3 c4 4. e4#

1. Rd6 Ke4 2. Bc6+ Kf5 3. fxe3 g5 4. e4#

CGCP 01576

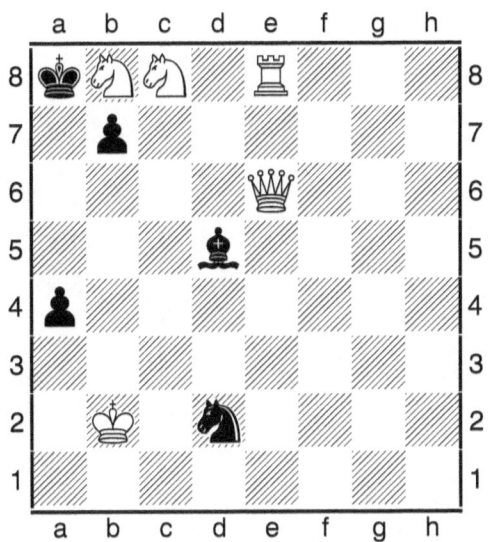

1. Nd6 a3+ 2. Kc2 Bb3+ 3. Qxb3 Nxb3 4. Nc6#

1. Nd6 a3+ 2. Kc2 Bb3+ 3. Qxb3 b6 4. Qa4#

1. Nd6 a3+ 2. Kc2 Bb3+ 3. Qxb3 b6 4. Qxa3#

1. Nd6 a3+ 2. Kc2 Bb3+ 3. Qxb3 a2 4. Qa3#

1. Nd6 a3+ 2. Kc2 Bb3+ 3. Qxb3 a2 4. Qxa2#

1. Nd6 a3+ 2. Kc2 Bb3+ 3. Qxb3 a2 4. Qxb7#

1. Nd6 a3+ 2. Kc2 Bxe6 3. Nc6+ Bc8 4. Rxc8#

1. Nd6 a3+ 2. Kc2 Ka7 3. Nb5+ Ka8 4. Na6#

1. Nd6 a3+ 2. Kc2 Ka7 3. Nb5+ Ka8 4. Nd7#

1. Nd6 Nc4+ 2. Kc3 Nb6 3. Nc6+ Nc8 4. Qxc8#

1. Nd6 Nc4+ 2. Kc3 Nxd6 3. Nc6+ Nxe8 4. Qc8#

1. Nd6 Nc4+ 2. Kc3 Nxd6 3. Nc6+ Nxe8 4. Qxe8#

1. Nd6 Nc4+ 2. Ka1 Nb6 3. Qxd5 a3 4. Qa5#

CGCP 01592

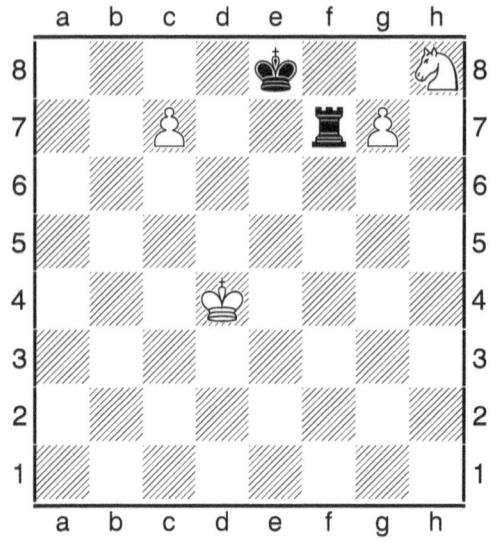

1. c8=Q+ Ke7 2. g8=N+ Kd6 3. Nxf7#

CGCP 01598

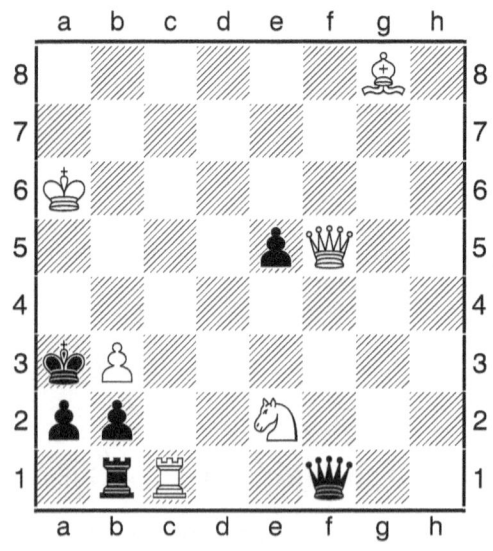

1. Rc4 Qf4 2. Qf8+ Qxf8 3. Ra4#

1. Rc4 Qf4 2. Qf8+ Kxb3 3. Qb4#
1. Rc4 Qf4 2. Nxf4 Kxb3 3. Qd3#
1. Rc4 Qf4 2. Nxf4 Kxb3 3. Qh3#
1. Rc4 Qf4 2. Rxf4 e4 3. Qa5#
1. Rc4 Qf4 2. Rxf4 e4 3. Qc5#
1. Rc4 Qf4 2. Rxf4 e4 3. Qf8#
1. Rc4 Qf4 2. Qxf4 Kxb3 3. Rc3#
1. Rc4 Qf4 2. Qxf4 Kxb3 3. Qe3#
1. Rc4 Qf4 2. Qxf4 Kxb3 3. Qf3#
1. Rc4 Qf4 2. Qxf4 Kxb3 3. Qg3#

CGCP 01601

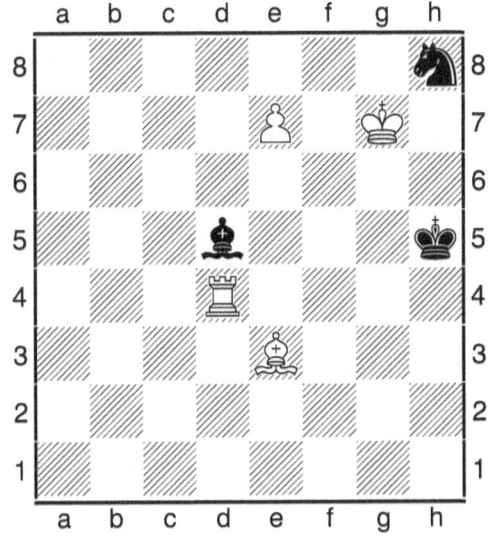

1. e8=N Be4 2. Rxe4 Nf7 3. Nf6#
1. e8=N Be4 2. Rxe4 Ng6 3. Nf6#

CGCP 01603

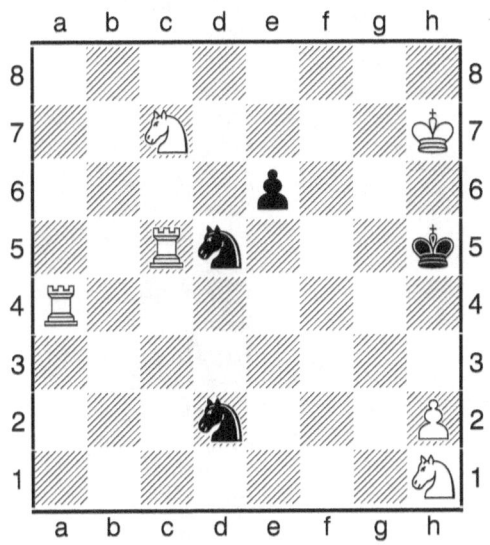

1. h4 Nc4 2. Raxc4 e5 3. Ng3#
1. h4 Nf1 2. Nxd5 e5 3. Nf6#
1. h4 Nf1 2. Nxd5 exd5 3. Rxd5#
1. h4 Nf1 2. Nxd5 Ng3 3. Nxg3#
1. h4 Nf1 2. Ne8 e5 3. Ng7#

CGCP 01606

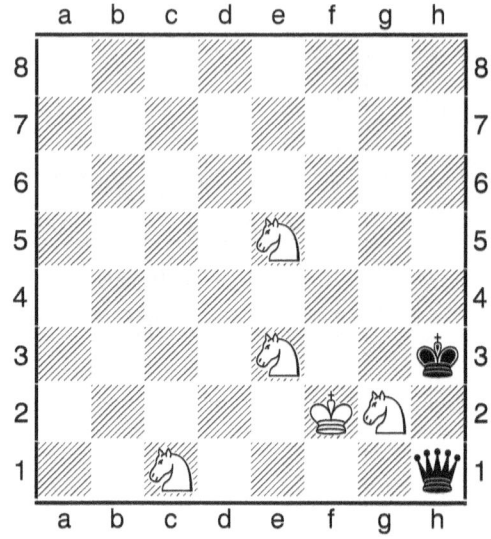

1. Ne2 Qxg2+ 2. Nxg2 Kh2 3. Ngf4 Kh1 4. Ng3+ Kh2 5. Nf3#
1. Ne2 Qg1+ 2. Nxg1+ Kh2 3. Nf1+ Kh1 4. Ng3+ Kh2 5. Ng4#
1. Ne2 Qg1+ 2. Nxg1+ Kh2 3. Nf5 Kh1 4. Ng3+ Kh2 5. Nef3#
1. Ne2 Qg1+ 2. Nxg1+ Kh2 3. Nf5 Kh1 4. Ng3+ Kh2 5. Ng4#
1. Ne2 Qg1+ 2. Nxg1+ Kh2 3. Nf1+ Kh1 4. Ng3+ Kh2 5. Nef3#
1. Ne2 Qxg2+ 2. Nxg2 Kh2 3. Ngf4 Kh1 4. Ng3+ Kh2 5. Ng4#
1. Ne2 Qh2 2. Ng1+ Qxg1+ 3. Kxg1 Kg3 4. Nf5+ Kh3 5. Nf4#

CGCP 01611

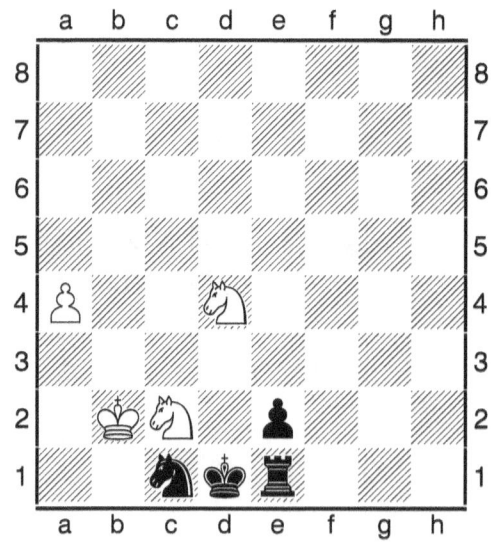

1. Nf3 Nd3+ 2. Kb1 Rf1 3. Ne3#
1. Nf3 Nd3+ 2. Kb1 Nb2 3. Ne3#
1. Nf3 Nd3+ 2. Kb1 Nc5 3. Ne3#
1. Nf3 Nd3+ 2. Kb1 Nc1 3. Ne3#
1. Nf3 Nd3+ 2. Kb1 Ne5 3. Ne3#
1. Nf3 Nd3+ 2. Kb1 Nf4 3. Ne3#
1. Nf3 Nd3+ 2. Kb1 Nf2 3. Ne3#
1. Nf3 Nd3+ 2. Kb1 Nb4 3. Ne3#
1. Nf3 Nd3+ 2. Kb1 Rg1 3. Ne3#
1. Nf3 Nd3+ 2. Kb1 Rh1 3. Ne3#

CGCP 01624

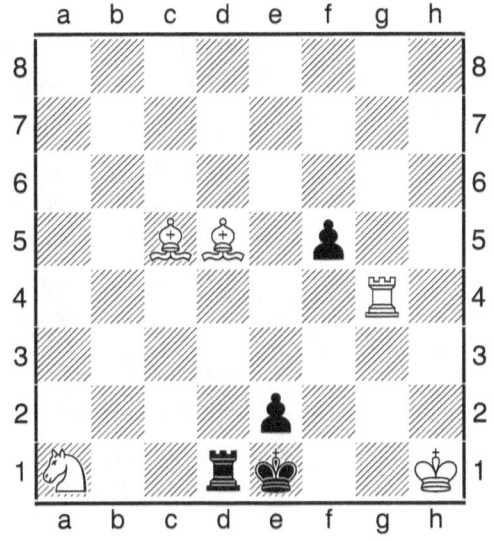

1. Be3 fxg4 2. Nc2+ Kf1 3. Bg2#

CGCP 01634

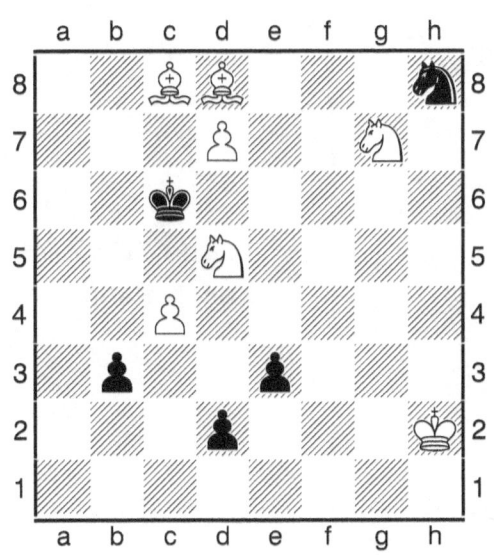

1. Be7 Nf7 2. Ne6 d1=Q 3. d8=N+ Nxd8 4. Nxd8#
1. Be7 Nf7 2. Ne6 d1=R 3. d8=N+ Nxd8 4. Nxd8#

CGCP 01635

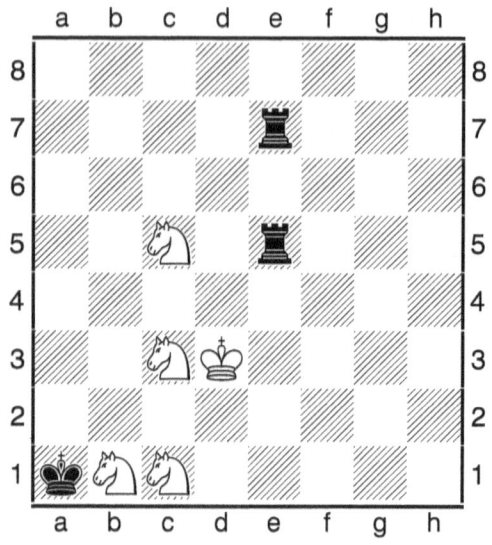

1. Kc2 Re2+ 2. N3xe2 Rb7 3. N5b3+ Rxb3 4. Nxb3+ Ka2 5. Nec3#
1. Kc2 Re2+ 2. N3xe2 Rxe2+ 3. Nxe2 Ka2 4. Nc1+ Ka1 5. N5b3#
1. Kc2 Re2+ 2. N3xe2 Rb7 3. N5b3+ Rxb3 4. Nxb3+ Ka2 5. Nec1#
1. Kc2 Re2+ 2. N3xe2 Rxe2+ 3. Nxe2 Ka2 4. Nec3+ Ka1 5. Nb3#

CGCP 01638

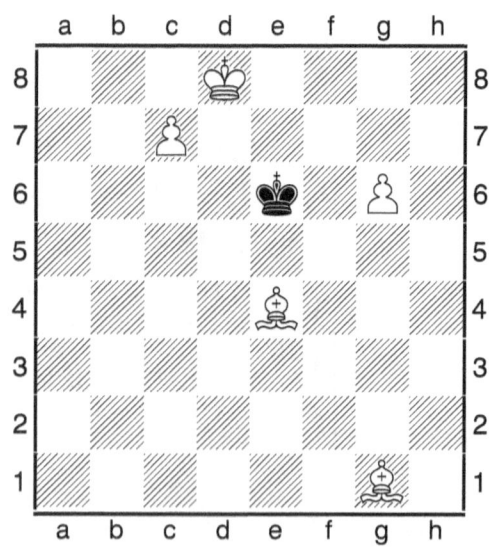

1. Bd4 Kd6 2. c8=R Ke6 3. Rc6#

CGCP 01646

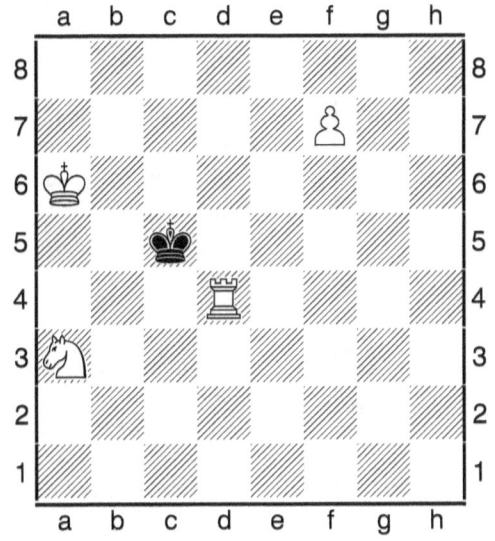

**1. Nb5 Kc6 2. f8=R
Kc5 3. Rc8#**

CGCP 01653

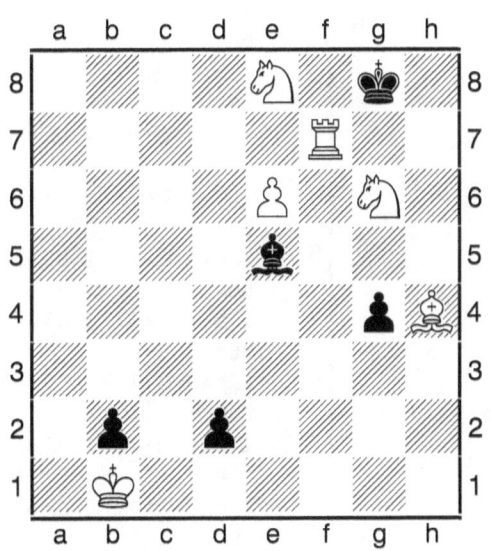

**1. Ne7+ Kh8 2.
Bf6+ Bxf6 3. Ng6+
Kg8 4. Nxf6#**

CGCP 01657

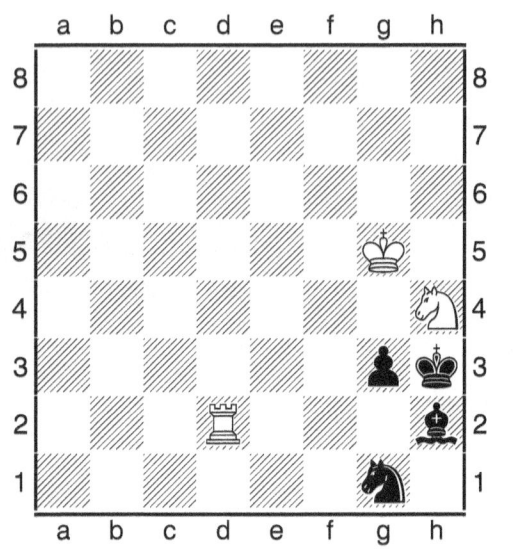

1. Ng2 Nf3+ 2. Kh5 Nxd2 3. Nf4#

1. Ng2 Nf3+ 2. Kh5 Nd4 3. Nf4#

1. Ng2 Nf3+ 2. Kh5 Ne5 3. Nf4#

1. Ng2 Nf3+ 2. Kh5 Ne1 3. Nf4#

1. Ng2 Nf3+ 2. Kh5 Ng5 3. Nf4#

1. Ng2 Nf3+ 2. Kh5 Ng1 3. Nf4#

1. Ng2 Nf3+ 2. Kh5 Nh4 3. Nf4#

1. Ng2 Nf3+ 2. Kh5 Bg1 3. Nf4#

1. Ng2 Ne2 2. Rxe2 Bg1 3. Nf4#

CGCP 01659

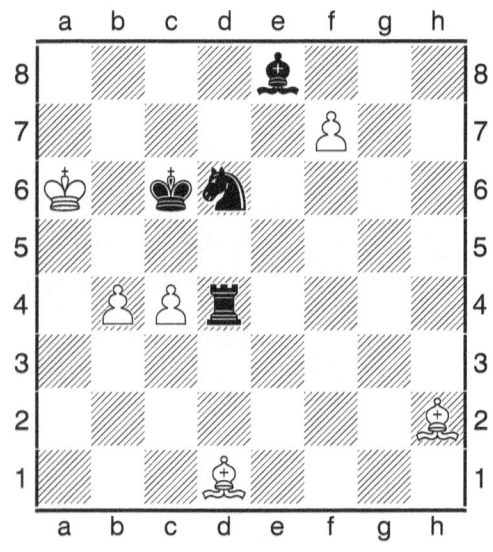

1. fxe8=Q+ Kc7 2. b5 Rxc4 3. b6#

1. fxe8=Q+ Kc7 2. b5 Rf4 3. b6#

1. fxe8=Q+ Kc7 2. b5 Rg4 3. b6#

1. fxe8=Q+ Kc7 2. b5 Rh4 3. b6#

1. fxe8=Q+ Kc7 2. b5 Re4 3. b6#

1. fxe8=Q+ Kc7 2. b5 Rd5 3. b6#

1. fxe8=Q+ Kc7 2. b5 Rd3 3. b6#

1. fxe8=Q+ Kc7 2. b5 Rd2 3. b6#

1. fxe8=Q+ Kc7 2. b5 Rxd1 3. b6#

CGCP 01672

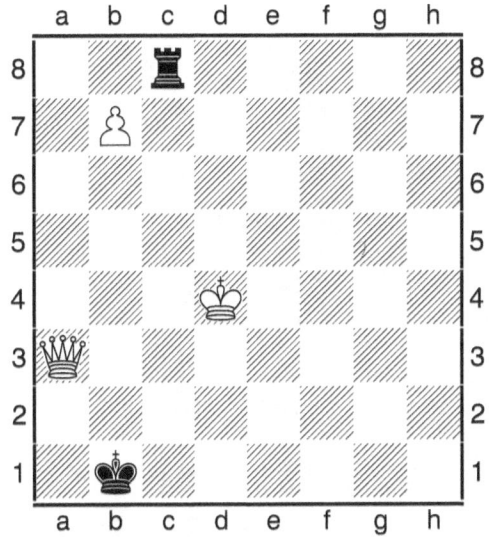

1. bxc8=B Kc2 2. Bg4 Kb1 3. Bf5#
1. bxc8=B Kc2 2. Bg4 Kd2 3. Qc3#

CGCP 01675

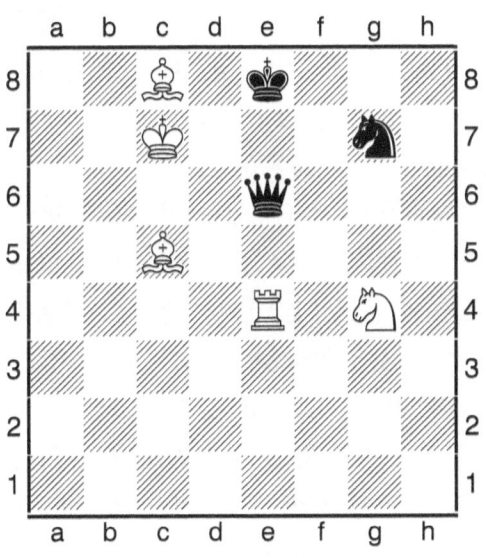

1. Nh6 Qe7+ 2. Rxe7+ Kf8 3. Re1#
1. Nh6 Qe7+ 2. Rxe7+ Kf8 3. Re6#
1. Nh6 Qe7+ 2. Rxe7+ Kf8 3. Re5#
1. Nh6 Qe7+ 2. Rxe7+ Kf8 3. Re4#
1. Nh6 Qe7+ 2. Rxe7+ Kf8 3. Re3#
1. Nh6 Qe7+ 2. Rxe7+ Kf8 3. Re2#
1. Nh6 Qe7+ 2. Bd7+ Kf8 3. Bxe7#
1. Nh6 Qe5+ 2. Rxe5+ Ne6+ 3. Rxe6#

CGCP 01700

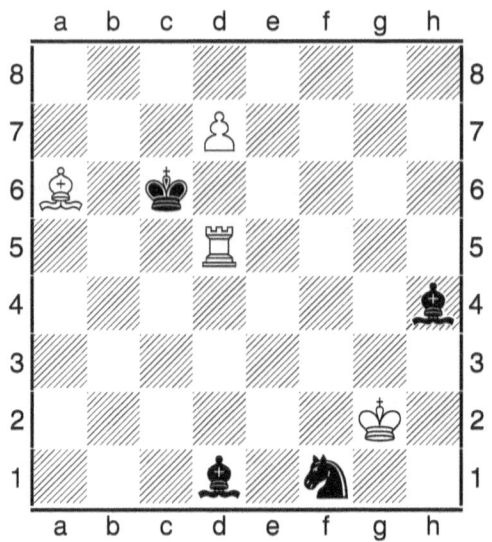

1. Kh3 Bd8 2. Rxd1 Ne3 3. Rd3 {Rd2 Kc7 Kg3 Nf5 Kf4 Nd6 Ke5 Nf7} **Nf5 4. Kg4 Nd6 5. Bc8 Nf7** {Be7 Rc3 Kd5 Re3 Bd8 Re8 Nf7 Kf5} **6. Kf5 Kc7 7. Rd1** {Ke6 Ng5 Ke5 Be7 Kf5 Bd8 Rg3 Nf7 Ke6} **Kc6** {Bh4 Ke6 Nd8 Kd5 Bg5 Rh1 Bd2 Rg1} **8. Ra1** {Ba6 Kc7 Be2 Bh4 Rh1 Bf2 Ke6 Nd8} **Kd6** {Bf6 Kxf6 Nd8 Ke7 Kc7 Rc1 Nc6 Rxc6 Kxc6} **9. Ra6+** {Rb1 Kc6 Rh1 Kc7 Ke6 Ng5 Ke5 Nf7} **Kc7** {Kc5 Rg6 Bh4 Ba6 Nd8 Bd3 Be1 Rf6 Kd4} **10. Ke6 Ng5+ 11. Kd5 Be7** {Nf7 Ra7 Kb6 Rb7 Ka5 Rb3 Bg5 Bb7} **12. Rc6+** {Ra7 Kb6 Rb7 Ka5 Rb3 Bd8 Bb7 Bc7} **Kd8 13. Rh6** {Rc4 Nf3 Rg4 Ng5 Kc6 Bf6 Rf4 Be7} **Nf7** {Kc7 Rg6 Nh7 Rg7 Nf6 Ke6 Bd8 Rg1} **14. Rg6** {Rh2 Ng5 Rh8 Kc7 Re8 Bf6 Re2 Nh7 Ke6} **Ng5 15. Rg8+** {Kc6 Nh7 Rg8 Nf8 Ba6 Bd6 Bd3 Be7} **Kc7 16. Re8 Bf6** {Bd8 Re1 Bf6 Re2 Nh7 Ke6 Bg5 Kf7} **17. Rg8** {Re2 Nh7 Ke6 Bh4 Rh2 Nf8 Kf7 Nxd7 Bxd7} **Be7** {Bd8 Rf8 Nh7 Rf2 Bg5 Ke6 Be3 Rh2 Nf8} **18. Re8 1-0**

CGCP 01703

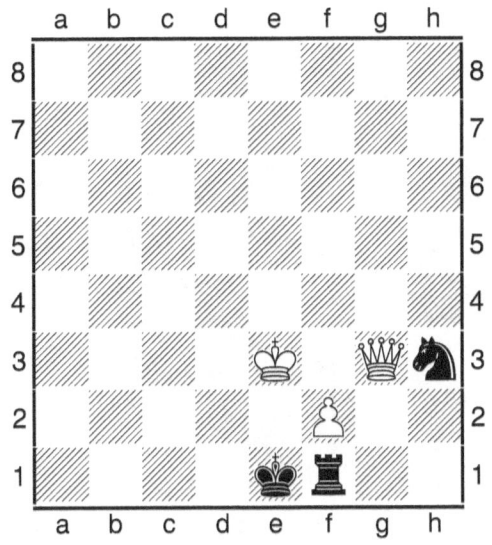

1. Qb8 Nxf2 2. Qb4+ Kd1 3. Qb1#
1. Qb8 Nxf2 2. Qb4+ Kd1 3. Qd2#

CGCP 01719

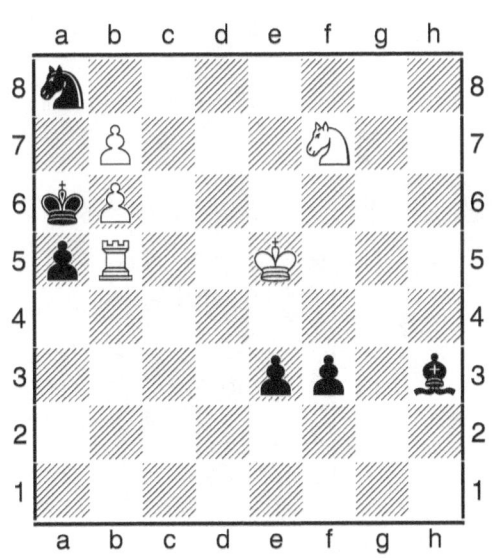

1. Nd6 Nxb6 2. b8=N+ Ka7 3. Nc6+ Ka6 4. Rxa5#
1. Nd6 Nxb6 2. b8=N+ Ka7 3. Nc6+ Ka8 4. Rxa5#

CGCP 01726

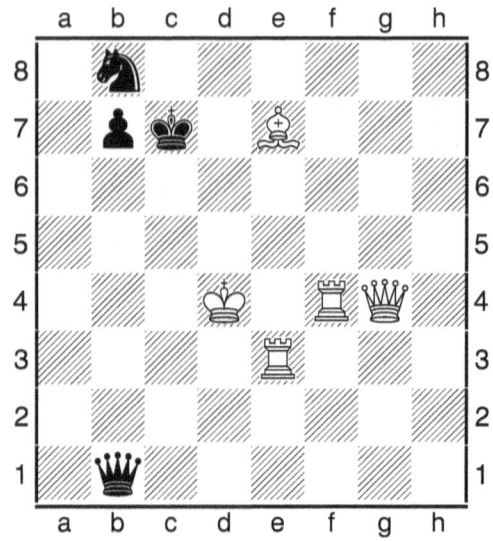

1. Bd8+ Kxd8 2. Rf8+ Kc7 3. Qc8+ Kb6 4. Qc5+ Ka6 5. Ra3#

CGCP 01729

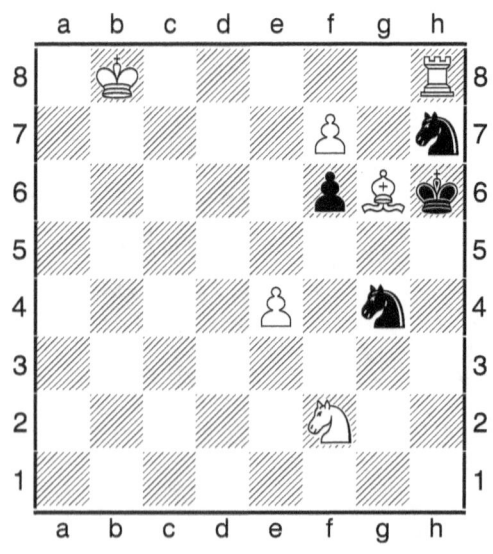

1. Rxh7+ Kxg6 2. f8=N+ Kg5 3. Nh3#
1. Rxh7+ Kg5 2. Nh3+ Kxg6 3. f8=N#

CGCP 01734

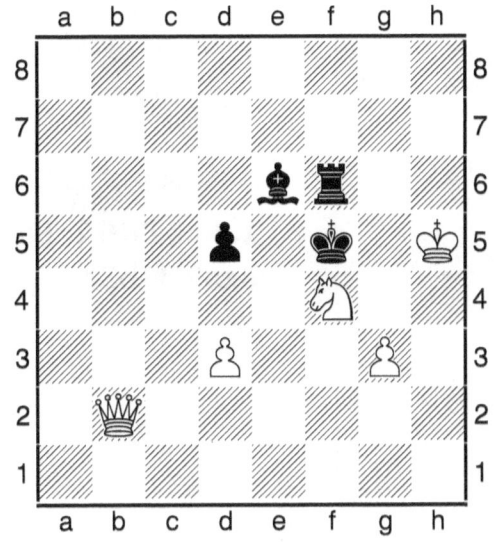

1. Ng6 Rxg6 2. Qf2+ Ke5 3. Qf4#

CGCP 01737

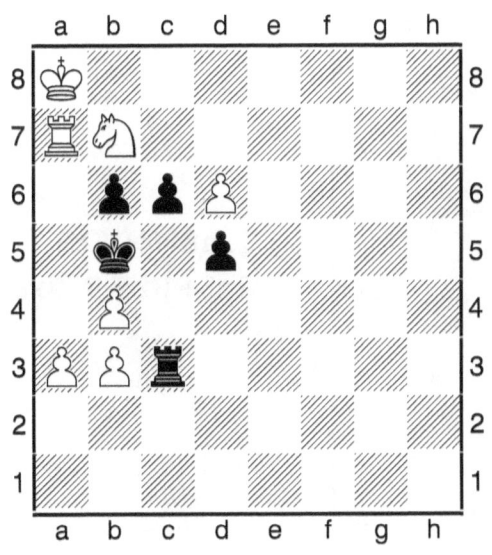

1. d7 c5 2. d8=N cxb4 3. a4#
1. d7 c5 2. d8=N c4 3. Nd6#

CGCP 01740

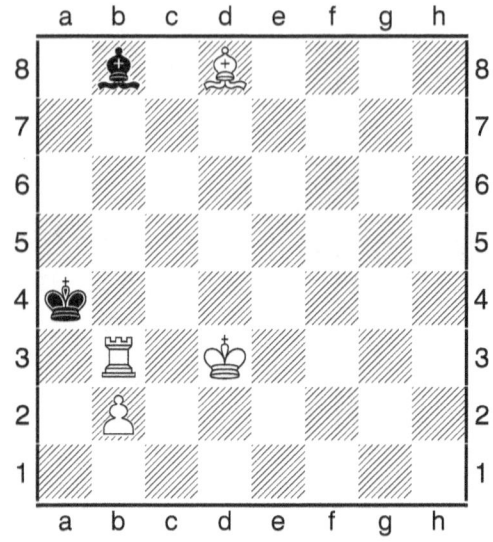

1. Kc4 Bd6 2. Ra3+ Bxa3 3. b3#

CGCP 01746

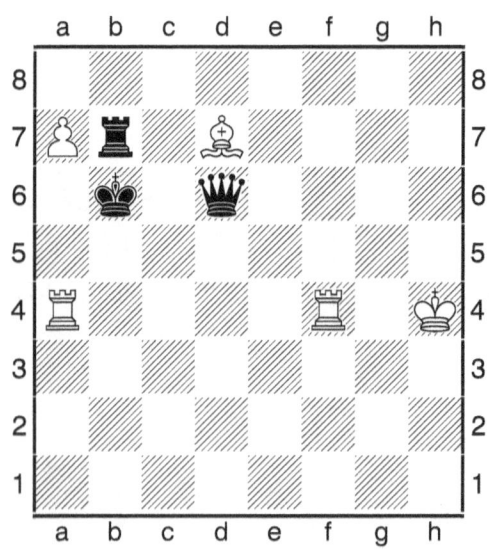

1. a8=N+ Kc5 2. Ra5+ Rb5 3. Rxb5#

CGCP 01747

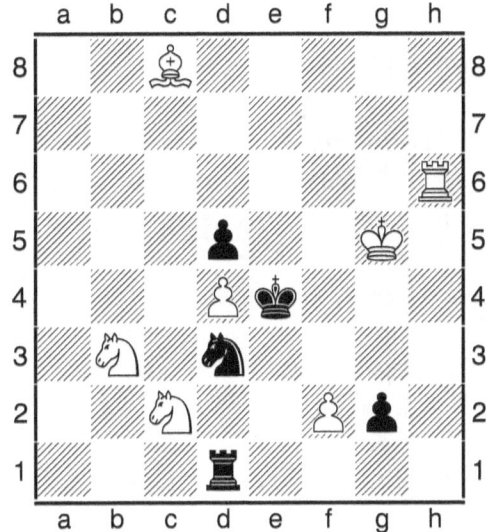

1. Bg4 g1=N 2.
Re6+ Ne5 3. Nc5#

REFERENCES

Additional Resources:

1. *Chesthetica.com*, Official Website.

2. *Computationally Estimating the Solvability of Forced Mate Sequences*, Figshare, York Way, London, United Kingdom, 25 June 2019, DOI: 10.6084/m9. figshare.8319881.

3. *Increasing Efficiency and Quality in the Automatic Composition of Three-Move Mate Problems*, in Entertainment Computing - ICEC 2011, Lecture Notes in Computer Science, Vol. 6972, pp. 186-197. Anacleto, J.; Fels, S.; Graham, N.; Kapralos, B.; Saif El-Nasr, M.; Stanley, K. (Eds.). 1st Edition., 2011, XVI. Springer. ISBN 978-3-642-24499-5.

4. *A Computer Composes A Fabled Problem: Four Knights vs. Queen*, arXiv, Cornell University Library, Cornell University, United States, 4 September 2017.

5. *Four Knights vs Queen Challenge*, ChessBase News, Hamburg, Germany, 8 September 2017.

6. *Four Knights vs Queen Challenge II*, ChessBase News, Hamburg, Germany, 2 October 2017.

7. *What Do People Really Find Attractive in Chess Problems?* ChessBase News, Hamburg, Germany, 10 February 2020.

8. *Can Computers Compose Artistic Problems? (Part 2)* ChessBase News, Hamburg, Germany, 16 June 2016.

Previous Books by Azlan Iqbal:

1. *Chesthetica's Book of Chess Constructs, Volume 3: Original Computer-Generated Chess Problems for Solving and Analysis*, Kindle Direct Publishing, Washington, United States, 2019, eISBN 978-983-808-248-8.

2. *Chesthetica's Book of Chess Constructs, Volume 2: Original Computer-Generated Chess Problems for Solving and Analysis*, Kindle Direct Publishing, Washington, United States, 2018, eISBN 978-983-808-246-4.

3. *Chesthetica's Book of Chess Constructs, Volume 1: Original Computer-Generated Chess Problems for Solving and Analysis*, Kindle Direct Publishing, Washington, United States, 2017, eISBN 978-983-808-244-0.

4. *The Digital Synaptic Neural Substrate: A New Approach to Computational Creativity*, 1st Edition, SpringerBriefs in Cognitive Computation, Springer International Publishing, Switzerland, 2016, eISBN 978-3-319-28079-0.

www.ingramcontent.com/pod-product-compliance
Lightning Source LLC
Chambersburg PA
CBHW030647220526
45463CB00005B/1676